Online Friendship, Chat-Room Romance and Cybersex

Your Guide to Affairs of the Net

Michael Adamse, Ph.D.
Sheree Motta, Psy.D.

Health Communications, Inc.
Deerfield Beach, Florida

Library of Congress Cataloging-in-Publication

Adamse, Michael, 1953-
  Online friendship, chat-room romance and cybersex: your guide to affairs of the Net / Michael Adamse, Sheree D. Motta.
    p.   cm.
  Includes bibliographical references.
  ISBN 1-55874-418-5 (trade paper)
  1. Friendship.   2. Information superhighway—Social aspects.   3. Internet (Computer network)—Social aspects.   4. Interpersonal communication.   5. Computer networks—Social aspects.   6. Online etiquette.   7. Computer sex.   I. Motta, Sheree D., 1962-   .   II. Title.
HM131.A298 1996   96-32715
025.06302—dc20   CIP

©1996 Michael Adamse and Sheree Motta
ISBN 1-55874-418-5 trade paper

All rights reserved. Printed in the United States of America. No part of this publication may be reproduced, stored in a retrieval system or transmitted in any form or by any means, electronic, mechanical, photocopying, recording or otherwise without the written permission of the publisher.

Publisher: Health Communications, Inc.
           3201 S.W. 15th Street
           Deerfield Beach, FL 33442-8190

Cover design by Andrea Perrine Brower

We dedicate this book
with much love to our parents,
Engel and Maria Adamse
and
Darrel and Gerry Clark

CONTENTS

Acknowledgments vii
Introduction ix
  1. Welcome to Cybercheers 3
  2. Personality in Cyberspace: Can't Leave Home Without It! ... 23
  3. Gender Gap on the Net 41
  4. Alt.Ego 61
  5. Friends and Support Online 77
  6. Romancing the Net 103
  7. Affairs of the Net 129
  8. Cybersex, Cybersex, Cybersex 149
  9. Caught in the Web 169
10. Beta Testing 189
Appendix: Self-Quiz 197
FAQs from Cyberspace 201
How It Works 215
Glossary 217
Emoticons 223
Acronyms 225
Bibliography 227
More Stories from the Net! 229

ACKNOWLEDGMENTS

Online Friendship, Chat-Room Romance and Cybersex: Your Guide to Affairs of the Net took six months to complete from initial conceptualization to finished manuscript. The pace was very rapid, not unlike the subject matter of the book itself. As with all creative endeavors, there are certain key people behind the scenes who provided us with the necessary guidance, support and encouragement that it takes to complete such a project. We are pleased to have the opportunity to thank them in print.

First and foremost, our heartfelt thanks to our publishers, Gary Seidler and Peter Vegso, who had the vision and faith to believe in us as *newbie* authors. When asked how they selected their books, Gary said, "We have a *feel* and a *sense* of who will do well." That will give you an idea of the kind of people they are.

Our great appreciation to Matthew Diener and Christine Belleris, our editors at Health Communications, whose professionalism and enthusiasm helped us every step of the way. To Randee Goldsmith and Kim Weiss, for their enthusiasm and support. To the rest of the staff at Health Communications, from creative design to those who run the printing press, we thank you.

To Jerry Smith (JC_), a special acknowledgment for all your online and offline support. Your efforts helped make this project so much easier. Not many people would cheerfully accept 3 A.M. conceptual and technical support questions.

To Gina Sanders, whose honest appraisal of our chapters and continual support helped guide our thinking and writing, and to

Karen Leeds, Steven Yellen, Andrea Appelman and Mary Mullen for their encouragement and support. And thanks to Dawn Goldberg for her hours of clerical assistance.

As for the many individuals whose stories brought the concepts we were illustrating to life, we are deeply grateful. The story behind Internet relationships was made *real* by your contributions.

We are indebted to our spouses Diane and Bob, and our children Elise, Dana, Sarah and Cosette who, we're sure, thoroughly understand the concept of being addicted to the Net. To those of you who are unnamed, we thank you as well.

INTRODUCTION

Great Expectations—Jan's Story

I am a 19-year-old freshman in college. I discovered the Internet about a month after I arrived in school. My best friend goes to school in another state, so we thought communicating online would be a great advantage for us. We decided to log onto the **Multi-User Dungeon (MUD)** so that we could talk. While I was there, I met many people from all over the world: males and females, old and young. I think MUDing is more of a college phenomenon though, so I did not meet many people past their late-20s.

I met many people with whom I quickly became friends. It is easy to open up to someone online because you don't have to look them in the face or see them the next day if you don't want. I still talk to many of the people I met in the beginning, and I even correspond via **"snail-mail"** with a few. Then, about two months ago, I met Hans on the MUD. Everyone had a made-up character and his in particular intrigued me.

We got to talking, and really enjoyed each other's company. Within a matter of days, we had confided some intimate things, spending up to three or four hours at a time talking per day. Soon after, we started exchanging pictures and

MUD. Multi-User Dungeon. Games played in real time on the Internet which involve multiple users who engage in adventure role-playing.

snail-mail. A term used in cyberspace to describe our conventional postal service delivery.

> **e-mail.** Electronically transmitted messages traveling from one computer to another.

letters via snail-mail as well as **e-mail** *messages. One day, before the pictures had arrived in the mail, he asked me to "go steady" with him in real life. I accepted immediately even though I had never seen his face. I felt a very special bond with him that I had never felt with anyone else before. Also, on the same day, he asked me to marry him on the MUD.*

So, now we are planning the wedding of our characters to each other. We have exchanged numerous packages and letters as well as some phone calls. He has booked his flight so that he can meet me this summer. (He lives in Holland. I live in the U.S.) We are both very excited because we think that we will have an even more wonderful relationship after we meet face-to-face.

My friends always ask if it is difficult dating someone I've never met. I don't think it is so hard. I know more about my boyfriend than some of them know about theirs, and they are with each other in person every day. My boyfriend and I really feel that we have a future together. Even though most people think relationships such as these don't work, we think we are proof that they do.

> **cyberspace.** A popular term used to describe the virtual meeting place of people who are using telecommunication technology.

This story is but one testament to the power of relationships online. What Jan shares in her story is expressed by many individuals who develop relationships in **cyberspace.** They describe a level of intimacy often not found in their real-life encounters. They describe a feeling of safety in letting their guard down, revealing vulnerabilities and feelings often not shared in real life. They also express a strong belief that the relationship will endure the distance between the modems that intimately connect them.

How can a virtual world created by technology and hardware become the hot, new social spot of the 1990s? Are relationships on the Net real? How can two people fall in love online? Can friendships on the Net be meaningful? Even though there are many skeptics who downplay the legitimacy of online relationships, the truth is that people *are* meeting people online. For the most part, relationships that solidify in cyberspace have tremendous value and meaning, perhaps more so than some relationships derived from real-life encounters.

Our project started with the development of Cybershrink (http://www.gate.net/~cyshrink or www.cybershrink.com), an online service offering psychological advice and education about relationships. Having been involved in private practice for many years, we felt it was time to explore other mediums by which we could educate people about maintaining healthy relationships. We received hundreds of e-mail questions from individuals in cyberspace who were confronting various relationship issues. To our surprise we found that many of these questions regarded relationships in which people were actively engaged online. So our work began.

We felt that the dynamics of two people meeting in a virtual world were unique and worthy of psychological understanding. Our interest in online services and expertise as psychologists seemed a

cybernauts. A term used to describe the people who are interacting on the Internet.

Webaholics. A person who is addicted to Internet usage. A webaholic may experience a need to spend increasingly longer periods online that may interfere with social or occupational functioning.

Cybercheers. A term we coined to capture the true spirit of cyberspace. to describe the spirit of the space behind your computer.

perfect combination for examining the social phenomenon taking place in this virtual world. Following hundreds of hours of online chat, observation and interviews with fellow **cybernauts**, we were able to shed some light on the many powerful connections taking place in cyberspace.

In our journey we heard so many stories that reflected the intensity of human emotion online. We have included several of these stories to bring concepts to life and to enhance the reader's understanding of the depth of interpersonal exchanges taking place. The stories are rich and expressive. We have changed all identifying information, including screen names, to protect confidentiality.

Our book invites you to take a careful look at the minds of individuals who venture through cyberspace in search of romance, sex, friendship and support. We have written it for anyone interested in navigating through cyberspace with a more sophisticated psychological understanding of cyber-relationships. From novice online users to weary-eyed **Webaholics** who chat around the clock, our book offers you professional insight into your online behaviors.

We start our journey with a great big "Welcome to **Cybercheers**!" In our first chapter we explore the setting of Cybercheers and discuss why it has become such a popular hang-out spot for cybernauts around the world. We talk about the type of patrons who hang out there and what makes communication in this setting so unique. Cybercheers isn't a physical setting. There are no floors, walls, cciling or bar stools for that matter, but Cybercheers does exist in the minds of online users.

Next, in Personality in Cyberspace, we take a peek at several types of personalities that cruise cyberspace: lurkers, narcissists, sociopaths, dependents, flamers and cybersocialites. We analyze each personality type and discuss what they are searching for in their online encounters. We challenge you to "shrink" your own personality in hopes of better understanding your journey online.

If you think we are all genderless in cyberspace, we have news for you: It is not so. Our Gender Gap chapter highlights the differences between men and women in this virtual world. Your gender does influence what you experience online. This chapter takes a careful look at what men and women are searching for when they enter the cybersocial arena. We also highlight differences in the way men and women communicate as they sit snuggled behind their computers. The chapter ends with a discussion of the ever popular cross-gender role-playing.

Our next chapter, Alt.Ego, takes a close look at the formation of **alter egos** in cyberspace. The Internet is a great equalizer that does not deny participation to anyone because of their sex, religion, race, age or income level. The anonymity allows for tremendous freedom of expression. With this freedom there is a tendency for many cybernauts to distort actual personality traits or personal information. Here we analyze why people

alter ego. A misrepresentation of actual factual personal data or personality characteristics.

project alter egos in cyberspace, and we also look at some of the potential problems regarding this phenomenon. We present case examples to illustrate people's alter egos.

Friends and Support Online takes a look at several heartwarming, first-person stories that depict the benevolent spirit often encountered in cyberspace. A woman who suffers the complexities of a multiple personality disorder and a man diagnosed with a rare medical condition find the support they are seeking in their online experiences. The inspiration and hope expressed in these online relationship stories will move you.

Next, we explore the power of love online in Romancing the Net. The first-person stories included in this chapter emphasize the intensity of romantic exchanges on the Net. Some stories are disappointing. Some are incomplete. Just like real life, some stories have a happy ending. You can judge for yourself how powerful the explosion of online romance truly is!

In our journey to understand the full range of relationships that develop online, the number of individuals engaging in **cyberaffairs** especially intrigued us! Affairs of the Net challenges the reader to consider whether cyberaffairs count as real-life affairs. We look at what makes flings on the Net so appealing and what are some of the potential risks of engaging in these relationships.

Cybersex, Cybersex, Cybersex: this chapter will certainly capture your attention! If you don't believe it happens, read and find out more about

cyberaffair.
A virtual affair.

this thing called **cybersex.** We start with a simple definition and end with some of the dangers of engaging in sexual play online. The chapter also looks at some of the benefits of people experimenting with their sexuality in this virtual world. The truth is that the anonymity of being online gives many people the opportunity to delve into their most private, erotic thoughts. We include case examples to illustrate the significance of these exchanges, along with actual typed text from a cybersexual encounter!

cybersex. Online equivalent of engaging in sex in the real world. Individuals type out their sexual fantasies for the purpose of mutual stimulation.

Feeling like you might be Caught in the Web? Believe it or not, many Net users are. In this chapter we explore the phenomenon of online addiction. We analyze why online services can easily become addictive and include a behavioral check list that will allow you to assess whether you have become a Webaholic. We also review four personality types (guidance seekers, social seekers, catharsis seekers and control seekers) that are prone to online addiction. We include case examples to demonstrate these types.

Our final chapter, Beta Testing, challenges the reader to think ahead in this virtual world. As the Internet expands, the world continues to shrink. Online services have no cultural limitations. People all over the world are connecting in powerful ways. As technology continues to evolve, the rules of behavior in virtual space will evolve as well. Navigate any time you wish, but be prepared to encounter challenging interpersonal experiences along the way.

Finally, in a special appendix we include a self-quiz to assess your level of interest in online relationships.

In reading this book you will find that it is our professional opinion that the good in cyberspace far outweighs the bad. Fear and distrust often accompany change, especially when it involves such a powerful communication medium as the Internet. Many individuals unfamiliar with the workings of Net relationships summarily condemn them or view those who engage in online socialization as "weird" in some way. One of the objectives of this book is to demystify the world of cyber-relationships and give the reader greater insight into the people who connect in cyberspace.

At the same time, users of the Internet need to approach online relationships with cautious optimism and a special sensitivity to the fact that there are concerns about young people who travel into cyberspace. Adults need to supervise children and adolescents online. We encourage online users to always consider that many children are navigating in cyberspace, pretending to be older and wiser than they are. Responsible and moral behavior is just as important in this virtual land as it is in real life.

It is also our finding that most people online are honest in what they communicate. Some people are looking for friendship and support. Others are looking for love. Many individuals start out seeking a casual connection and end up falling in love. In our journey to understand relationships as they exist in cyberspace, we found many people who have had their lives enriched by their relationships online.

Years of practice in our profession as psychologists have reinforced our observation that intimate relationships don't come easily. For many, the world has become an unsafe place in which to meet and connect. Cyberspace allows us to venture out in a convenient and safe way. For this reason, we extend to you a "Welcome to Cybercheers!"

SHARON'S STORY

My name is Sharon. I am a 32-year-old woman, living in Kansas. I have been married, mostly happily, for 11 years and have a 6-year-old daughter. Pieter is 35 and lives with his wife of three years and his small son (two years old) in a village in Scotland. We have never met face to face, but have been in love with each other for a year now.

In February of 1994, I was a housewife with a need to reach out to the world. I feel I have the best job ever: taking care of my family. I do it well and with relish, but I suffered from the natural isolation that being a full-time mother can impose. I very strongly felt the need to reach out to the world. Having little time, energy and, frankly, the desire it requires to make more close friendships outside the home than I already have, the Internet seemed an ideal solution. I could be in contact with the world, in a broad sense, through e-mail, **newsgroups** and the **World Wide Web (WWW)**. I could also be in more immediate contact with people through the **Internet Relay Chat (IRC)** forum. I could get on the Net in my bathrobe in the mornings, drinking coffee and looking as sleepy as I wanted, and I could disappear whenever I felt like it . . .

1

Welcome to Cybercheers

David and Eric live in a major city and have been friends for years. They've been through many good times together and a few bad ones too. Throughout it all, their friendship has been an anchor and a reference point on which they both could count. Their lives and busy schedules make it hard to get together but somehow they manage to meet now and again at a favorite pub.

Eric has a lot on his mind lately and could use a good ear. He's been meaning to get together with David for a while, but something always seems to prevent it. They finally decide to meet after work one evening and catch up. When David and Eric stroll into their local hangout, they take refuge in a place that's familiar and, for the most part, friendly. They go over to their favorite seats at the bar and exchange a few words with the bartender. Then, Eric unloads his troubles. David listens carefully and offers some encouraging words. Eric drives home feeling better for having shared his troubles, but also a little frustrated that they don't get to see each other more often. He misses their time together.

Welcome to Cybercheers

PC. Refers to the personal computer which is the basic hardware permitting the average individual to gain access to cyberspace.

chat room. A virtual room in cyberspace where individuals "gather" to discuss certain themes. Chat rooms can include as many as 20 or more people.

LOL. Cybershorthand for laughing out loud.

Elsewhere in the same city, Peter comes home from a demanding day at the office, grabs a snack from the fridge, and says hi to his wife and kids. He tells his wife he'll be out in about an hour and then goes into his study, flips on the **PC** and signs on as "Bps." He joins an Internet **chat room,** 40 Something, and says hi to the group. Tim, a 40 Something regular, lives about 3,000 miles away and goes by the screen name "Dutch." He asks Peter how the project at work is going and if he's still worried about the company downsizing. Peter unloads for a while and has a private chat with Tim.

Bps: *Yeah, they're talking about laying off another 300 people . . . technical and support.*

Dutch: *When?*

Bps: *Within the next few months . . . no one knows exactly.*

Dutch: *You affected?*

Bps: *About 20 or so in my group . . . no one knows who's going to be "surplused."*

Dutch: *I think "surplused" is corporate jargon for "screwed" . . .* **LOL.**

Bps: *It's like a terrorist bomb . . . don't know where it's going to explode or whom it's going to kill!*

Dutch: *Yeah buddy, but at least you know it's coming . . . need to work on a contingency plan.*

Bps: *You got that right. Mortgage. Car payments. College for the kids. Prospect of no income after working for this company the last 16 years? What's wrong with this picture?*

Dutch: *It's tough. You'll be OK. For now, let me buy you a* **cyberdrink** *. . . mmmmm . . .*

Bps: *Hits the spot . . . (toast)*

cyberdrink. An imaginative drink shared in cyberspace.

After all, Tim knows where he's coming from: He was laid off himself after 26 years at a major corporation. Peter feels better for having shared with someone who has no strings attached. He can and does talk to his wife, but he doesn't want her to worry. Peter and Tim have been online friends for a long time. They've spent many hours chatting about family, sports, politics, women. They've never had an opportunity to meet nor have they even spoken on the phone. Nevertheless, they do have an intimate connection.

Welcome to Cybercheers!

Cybercheers isn't a physical setting. There are no walls, floors or ceilings to define the space, no barstools, no street address. People wander in and out, some staying for a moment, others for hours. No one has to travel to get there. In fact, the members of a particular "room" are usually scattered all over the country or all over the world for that matter. Time and distance are no obstacles to connecting. The architects of the Internet have created a place to connect minds, not bodies.

Cybercheers exists in cyberspace, and cyberspace exists in the mind of the user. You won't find anyone behind your computer screen, just a bunch of sophisticated circuitry. Yet, as millions of users do every minute of every day, belief suspends reality and it doesn't really matter. What matters is that we "believe" it exists and, more important, we believe the contact we make with others on the Internet—in all of its forms—is every bit as real as real life.

The Internet phenomenon of chat rooms is explosive in its popularity. There are many hundreds of rooms available to the **Netsurfer.** These rooms are organized around some general themes reflecting the tone of each room or the interests of the participants. Our friend Peter doesn't have just a few choices about where to go to connect in cyberspace. He has hundreds of sites from which to choose. He can move from room to room in seconds as he searches for a conversation that interests him. If he decides he wants to get to know someone better, he can simply **IM** them or check their **profile.**

Just like real-world hot spots, during peak hours it can be difficult to join one's favorite room. Some Cybercheers patrons will try persistently to get in and can only do so when a fellow cybernaut decides to leave. Timing is important. Why would anyone want to work to get into a room where all they're doing is typing back and forth? To understand the appeal of Cybercheers, we need simply understand an aspect of basic human nature.

Human beings have a basic need to connect with others and make sense of their lives. We are social beings. As society continues to suburbanize and we

Netsurfer. An individual who most often cruises cyberspace with no particular destination in mind.

IM. Instant message. Refers to a private message sent to someone which is received immediately while online.

profile. Select internet providers allow individuals to post personal information such as age, gender, interests, etc., for others to view.

become increasingly removed from our neighbors, we behave in direct conflict to this aspect of our basic natures. The frenetic pace of life for many of us reduces our contact to brief sound bites that have little or no meaning. The garage door opener lets us pull our cars into the garage without getting out, which gives us an excuse not to say hello to our neighbors. Many of us are burned out by the end of the day and don't want to deal with anyone.

This situation leads to a contradiction. We often want to get away from others and be close to them at the same time. Cybercheers is another way to satisfy our need for connection. The relationships formed there can range from casual and fleeting to serious and life-long. Patrons of Cybercheers enjoy it and if they don't, they don't have to participate. Venturing into the world of cyberspace relationships is a choice we're making in record numbers. To get a better idea of the kinds of intimate connections taking place in Cybercheers, let's float around some rooms and get a sample.

Jerry (JC_) in Texas works as a detective. He spends his days dealing with the various stresses that police work brings with it. By the end of his shift he's frequently had it. He's tired and burned out and sits down with a cold beer in front of his PC and joins an Internet chat room called COPS. There he talks with Super Cop out of San Francisco; Koala, a police officer in Sydney; and FancyJane, a police groupie out of Baltimore. These are all regulars whom he knows after months of conversing online.

He immediately feels at home, connected with others who know just how he feels. He tells them he's had a hard day. They commiserate around their terminals, just as our ancestors did around a campfire after the day's hunt or a day spent tilling the land. JC_'s experience reveals a deeper truth: the need to be connected to others who can understand where he's coming from. It helps to know that cops in Australia can get as stressed out at times as cops in America. There are millions of JC_s out there in cyberspace.

Susan (Baygirl) lives in the bay area of San Francisco and has always had difficulty with shyness and discomfort in social arenas. She functions very well in the work environment, which dictates the rules of behavior and gives them structure and clarity. However, in social settings she always feels anxious and fears that others will not like her or will find her boring and uninteresting. As with many individuals who are shy, Susan avoids get-togethers to avoid the risk of rejection.

Alt.groups. bulletin boards in cyberspace containing posted messages relevant to the topic of the group.

While surfing the Net one evening, she came across an **Alt.group** that listed postings containing information about her problem: Alt.Shyness. There she found several postings on a cyber-bulletin board containing information and suggestions on how to deal with her shyness. She realized that she was far from alone and that many others like herself suffered from shyness. More important, Susan felt a deep sense of relief in knowing that she was not weird, nutty or crazy. After all, we're all human and scared of something.

Someone suggested through a posting that a chat room existed with members who had a common problem with shyness. Susan decided to try it. After all, what was the worst that could happen? If she felt too uncomfortable she could just click out of the room! Over the next few weeks and months, Baygirl would "drop by" this room and visit for an hour or so chatting with various friends she had met online. Those in the room—Morgen in New York City, Jace24 in Los Angeles, Webmeister in Germany and others—greeted her the moment she signed on, and soon became familiar with the current happenings in her life. The content of these chats rarely had to do with shyness directly as a topic of discussion. Shyness was the common denominator, not the preoccupation. There is comfort in familiarity and security in acceptance.

Susan's experiences on the Net greatly enhanced her confidence in her ability to socialize. The text-driven nature of the medium encouraged her to better articulate herself. She learned that the more effectively you learn to communicate, the more confident you become. Susan became more self-assured outside the Net as well, and started accepting invitations to socialize.

Individuals who have not experienced chat rooms may be skeptical of the ability to connect with others in any kind of a meaningful way. They may conclude that cyberspace is for people who can't relate in the real world and that the Net undermines rather than enhances social interaction. We haven't found that to be the case. Although one can develop an addiction to the Net, our experience indicates that the vast majority of people who relate online have very full lives offline. For them, the chat rooms provide another convenient and fun medium to connect with others around the country or around the world. Relationships forged on the Net are quite real and very meaningful for many. Text-based interactions frequently lead to exchanges of **GIFs** and phone calls. Phone calls lead to visits, or perhaps a party for the chat room. Many romances begin online and sometimes result in marriage.

GIFs. Graphic interchange format; pictures sent over the Internet.

The modem and the 24-hour-a-day nature of the Net make going online convenient and accessible to almost everyone. It also permits contact with others at virtually any time and place. Cybercheers doesn't close down and you don't have to travel to get there. In addition, chat rooms allow the user to interact with many others at the same time. Some rooms have upwards of 20 members or more. These individuals move in and out of the stream of dialog, participating or simply observing. Diane is an example of someone who appreciates the convenience of the Internet.

Diane (Di'sPlace) has been a regular in several chat rooms that cater to romance. She visits several an evening in what she calls "cyber room-hopping," similar to bar-hopping but minus the need for a designated driver. She enjoys it and has made many online friends, some of whom she has met in person. Diane's career required her to move from Miami to a smaller city in western Kentucky. By simply subscribing to a local server, she was able to resume her relationships on the Net without interruption. Diane didn't have to give up her friends online. In the world of cyberspace, it doesn't matter where you hook up your modem.

Your station in life also doesn't matter. No social stratum exists in Cybercheers; everybody really is the same. The Net levels the playing field. Social status doesn't matter. Income is irrelevant. It doesn't matter if you're sitting in front of your PC in an Armani suit or naked. Race and creed are unimportant. This is the true revolution of the medium. Cybercheers doesn't judge anyone at the door so long as they are using proper **Netiquette.** It is an extremely egalitarian medium in the social psychological sense. What *does* count is creativity, wit and a sense of speed, as text can move very quickly on the Net, especially in active chat rooms. Bob's and Susan's cyberspace connection illustrates how relationships can develop on this level field.

Bob (Cybrguy) from Chicago is five feet, six inches tall, weighs 265 pounds and is nearly bald. Megan (Netbabe) is five feet, four inches tall, weighs 120 pounds and is very attractive. Appearances count very heavily in initial social interactions. We assume perceived attractiveness corresponds to likability. In Cybercheers it doesn't matter what you look like, at least initially. Bob and Megan have been friends on the Net for over a year and they regularly share what's going on

Netiquette. The use of Net-specific manners while online.

in their lives. If they had met in real life, they may or may not have ever connected. Bob reports that he never would have approached Megan in real life because he would have feared rejection. Megan says she would have been unlikely to respond to Bob because he isn't her type. They both agree that their friendship developed in Cybercheers—where appearances don't count for much and language counts for almost everything—in a way that never would have in a real-world setting.

On the Net, a line from a Cybercheers theme song might be, "And everybody knows your thoughts." When someone in a real-life setting makes a comment, he generally directs it to one or perhaps a few individuals. In Cybercheers, what you say is being seen by upwards of 20 or more individuals, unless you're in a private chat. Just as in any social gathering, the range of conversation is limitless and runs the gamut from boring to stimulating, depending on taste. The difference is that there is no way to whisper or to deny what you said. Once you've said something, it's "out there" in black and white.

Our friends David and Eric may say something that's overheard by someone else at the pub. Say Eric makes a less than complimentary comment about the intellectual prowess of bikers only to find that a biker is next to him at the bar. Our biker friend may ask Eric to repeat what he said, giving Eric a chance to clean it up. Eric may get away with a second, more carefully considered response. That doesn't happen in Cybercheers. You can't pull it back and the reader gets to go over it as many times as he or she wants. There is one safeguard, however. The Net permits the user to remain anonymous: He need not reveal anything about himself. If you mess up, who's going to really know? Psychologically, the anonymity of the Net is a double-edged sword.

On the one hand, not having to reveal any true identifying features of oneself allows an individual to interact or observe a group without pressure to perform or impress. For example, a heterosexual person who has some curiosity about homosexual persons might decide to observe a gay and lesbian chat room. Familiarity reduces anxiety and such an experience may contribute to an attitude shift in which our observer decides that relationship issues are pretty much the same no matter what a person's sexual orientation.

On the other hand, the opportunity to misrepresent oneself is obvious. Do you really know the age, sex and occupation of the individual with whom you are connecting? Is the information being revealed to you the truth, a lie or an exaggeration? The risks for certain types of distortions are greater on the Net than in real life given that the only clues available to you are those generated by text. In a real-life setting, you have much more information with which to evaluate others. Intuition has to work harder over the Internet.

What drives individuals to distort? The same reason people distort in real life: insecurity, a fear of rejection, a need to be accepted and selfishness. The *good news* is that the vast majority of Internet users engaging in online relationships are honest and just being themselves. They report that the Net allows them to let their guard down and have fun connecting. These cybernauts will reveal more of their personal feelings and details about their personal lives as they get to know a group or individual better. Trust and a need for security extend into cyberspace. The *bad news* is that there are plenty of alter egos in cyberspace who raise BS stories to an art form. Still, Cybercheers can be a liberating place.

Cybercheers provides many individuals with an opportunity to express thoughts and feelings that they would otherwise suppress. The forum of the chat room gives an individual the license to say what's on her mind with less concern for how others will react. Alt.groups are an even easier form of expression because responses to thoughts and opinions are not as immediate. The Internet allows and even encourages individuals to open up in ways that perhaps they never would have in real life. Chat rooms are a great place to meet and have fun, but they are also a source of tremendous encouragement and support, as Richard discovered.

Richard (Alex 212) is a very successful and prominent attorney who is active in a number of social organizations in town. He is well-liked and enjoys respect among his peers. Richard is married, has two children, attends church regularly and is considering running for local office. He is also an active alcoholic who needs help and he knows it. He has considered therapy, rehab and AA, but is concerned about his privacy. Even more important for Richard is his pride. He is a proud man and feels shame due to his behavior, even though he intellectually understands it's a problem shared by millions of people.

About six months ago, Richard joined the group "Friends of Bill W" on the Internet. For the first time in 14 years of secretly struggling with this problem, he admitted his alcoholism and asked for help. No one in the room knows his true identity and he feels safe there. Richard has experienced a great deal of support from many of the regulars and others in the group. When he finds himself struggling with the desire to drink, meetings are only a keyboard away. In Richard's case, Cybercheers has nothing to do with pouring a drink and everything to do with preventing it.

There are all kinds of relationships in cyberspace: friendships, romances, sexual relationships. With these relationships come love, affection, erotic arousal, intrigue, anticipation, excitement, anger, disappointment, intellectual stimulation, and even boredom; the full range of emotions that comes with being uniquely human. Fascinating as it is, the real story behind the explosive growth of the Internet isn't really the technology. The real story is about the people who use it to connect intimately.

Paul's View

Paul lives in London and has recently experienced a love affair over the Internet that has been a source of both happiness and frustration. His view of Cybercheers provides us with a good starting point of what it's like to venture into the world of intimate connections in cyberspace.

I admit getting a certain buzz out of meeting people online. Mostly, one becomes good friends with people and the relationship remains confined to e-mail. Occasionally, it is possible to meet people with the same interests as you who are looking for similar things, i.e., close friendship, companionship or even love.

I have always found it very easy to meet new people using the Internet. If, like myself, people use an Internet service provider the procedures involved are very user-friendly and easy to master. At first, I was very nervous and just "lurked" in forums, choosing not to talk to people but to listen to their conversations. Eventually, someone did choose to talk to me. I can describe it as being at a party where you know nobody. Eventually, someone sees you and decides to talk. Conversations can last anywhere from five minutes to several hours. The longest conversation I have had with someone lasted four hours! There is also a thrill in talking with someone on the other side of the world in real time. I think this is the most appealing aspect.

On the whole, people should enter into Internet relationships with a very open mind, hoping for the best, aware that they may be disappointed, and taking what comes!

Welcome to Cybercheers!

SHARON'S STORY (Continued)

I began to explore my long-hidden sexual desires with my husband, who was a little freaked out by them. I had discovered a year or so before that I was far more interested in BDSM [bondage/discipline, sadomasochism] than in "vanilla sex" (straight sex). This was a frightening realization for me. I knew no one who liked this, and found that most people thought it sick. I realized I had needs that were out of the mainstream when I was nine years old. I had suppressed these needs until somewhere around the age of 30, when they became impossible to ignore.

My marriage, though full of potential, had become unstable. One of the reasons was that years before I had given up on having sex because I found it dull and unfulfilling. I came to realize, much to my horror, that the reason for this was that my needs were going unspoken and therefore unmet.

On IRC, everything changed for me. I began to quietly frequent the BDSM chat rooms (we call them channels). Though I was terrified of myself—and of being caught by my husband—I was fascinated by the people and their openness, turned-on by the topics being discussed and dumbfounded at how totally *normal* everyone there seemed. I gradually moved into the community, hesitantly making friends. Telling my husband about this still frightened me, but many good people encouraged me to finally confront my fears *and* my husband. I was

SHARON'S STORY (Continued)

beginning to feel normal about my desires, and enjoyed the occasional "play scene" (Netsex or cybersex) with several channel members. It whetted my appetite. Finally, I sat down at the computer with my husband next to me, took a deep breath, and joined Spanking, my favorite channel. My husband sat with his jaw on the floor as many people greeted me by my nick (Judi), obviously knowing me and knowing about my husband. I talked to them for a long time that evening, while he watched. He never said a word the entire time, and I was trying to behave as though I was in a room like #chatzone or #FriendlyTalk.

Finally after about an hour of his silence, I looked over at him. He looked at me, then down at his lap, drawing my attention there. He was obviously aroused. I said a flurry of good-byes and we sprinted for the bedroom.

After that, I became totally free with my desires. Talking to others in these chat rooms opened a floodgate within me. In my mind I explored long-buried desires and needs that had seemed shameful and a source of humiliation for me before.

2

Personality in Cyberspace: Can't Leave Home Without It!

When venturing into cyberspace, you really can't leave your personality behind. Even alter egos have their origin in the psyches of the individuals who invent them. Your activity in the world of the Internet is an extension of your attitudes, beliefs and self-image. You are what you type and you can't deny that. While every person is unique, there are some general groupings that emerge.

These personality types really reflect subgroups of users as the Internet attracts a heterogeneous population representing all types of people. The vast majority of cybernauts are normal everyday individuals. Having said that, let's look at the types of people who cruise the Net, especially those you may want to avoid.

Shrinking the Lurker's Mind

Ever notice the people in the background of television bars and restaurants? The ones who set the backdrop for the story, but you never hear what they are saying? They are the "extras" whose role it is to help create the setting so that

lurker. A visitor to a newsgroup or online service who observes communication between others but doesn't participate.

newbie. A newcomer to cyberspace.

cyber-shorthand. Acronyms and emoticons used online in place of complete phrases or sentences, i.e., BRB—be right back, LOL—laughing out loud.

the main characters can strut their stuff. They are there in the room but not part of the action.

In Cybercheers there are plenty of extras who hang out in the virtual corners of various chat rooms. These **lurkers** are cybernauts who are present in the chat room but do not become active in any exchanges taking place there. They may never participate in a single exchange with another individual, yet they are there anyway, watching the chatting going back and forth. They may spend many hours simply observing. Often, a lurker will move quickly from room to room in search of something interesting. He is here one second, gone the next.

So, what's going on in the mind of these *virtual voyeurs* anyway? Why would they just watch the goings on instead of joining in?

Lurkers are really of three types. The first type is an individual who is simply new to the world of the Internet. He may feel unsure of what to say and how to say it. In the fast-moving rooms of Cybercheers, it can be quite intimidating to begin chatting when you seem to be in the company of veterans. It is sort of like walking into a bar for the first time and realizing everyone seems to know everyone else except for you. On top of that, Internet chatting has created a new language and the **newbie**, or beginner, is often seeing **cyber-shorthand** that's puzzling. God forbid she ask anyone what it means!

These lurkers usually check things out for a while before "taking the plunge." As they become more confident, they begin to participate more and more. Before they know it, they're Cybercheers regulars. Many times, someone encourages them to become involved by either greeting them in the room or IMing them. The majority of rooms are friendly places to be and there are many fellow cybernauts who encourage newbies to join in. It's hard to observe when someone just says hi to you.

Lurkers of the type just described are the most common found in cyberspace. They're mostly individuals who may be a bit reserved socially, or who find the new technology and everything they may have heard about the Net a little intimidating. Women, in particular, may be especially cautious because of reservations that men may be hitting on them. This lurker status is usually a temporary stage. Individuals rarely return to it once they have passed it.

The second type of lurker may never come out of the virtual closet. The individual who is always observing and never participating is more likely to be very shy or even avoid social contact. He may be uncomfortable in any social setting, even one as seemingly risk-free as the Internet. Fear of rejection or imagined criticism leads to avoidance. For these lurkers, the safest way to prevent evaluation of themselves is to remain quiet.

The third type of lurker simply enjoys observing as a form of entertainment, not unlike listening to the radio or flipping on the TV. Watching the flow of conversation going back and forth can be a relaxing diversion.

One last point about lurkers: They are not antisocial people. They're not weird or schizophrenic. They wouldn't be out there in the various chat rooms of the Internet at all if they didn't have an interest in people. Their presence is welcome. They should always remember that they can step up to the bar and start a chat anytime so the rest of us in Cybercheers can enjoy their company.

Shrinking the Flamer's Mind

flamers. Individuals who send nasty, insulting messages via e-mail or postings.

It is best to think of **flamers** as cyber party-poopers: individuals who insult others without provocation. Flamers use words as weapons to ridicule and criticize unfairly. An attack is usually sudden and unforeseen. Eavesdropping on Fred (Netter) provides a good example of a flamer. From a grandstand seat, we witness a flame attack from Fred on Mitch (Miner) and Roy (Richboy). Mitch and Roy are both in the chat room Current Affairs, exchanging their political views:

Miner: I think Clinton's decision to move into Bosnia was wise.
Richboy: You do, huh? Why?
Miner: He didn't really have a choice ... so many people dying ... no one taking the bull by the horns!
Richboy: I don't agree ... we're always getting sucked in ... need to push UN to increase their role.
Netter: You're both MORONS. Need to drop an atomic bomb and get it over with.

Miner: *Morons? Where do you get off with that?*

Netter: *Superior intellect that's where! You're probably two arm chair intellectuals who don't know your ass from your elbows . . . GO SCREW YOURSELVES!!! Have a nice day. :)*

It's unlikely Fred would have said that in a real-world setting. In cyberspace, people are less inhibited. They say things that others might respond to with a drink or punch in the face. There are no rules that prevent someone from being obnoxious. A flamer is free to be as rude as he likes with little or no consequence. Often, other cybernauts in the room will counter a flame with a flame, hence the term **flame war.** Unfortunately, this type of reaction is just what many of these individuals are looking for. The best response is none at all.

Flamers take pleasure in putting down others. As a rule, flamers are insecure people who have an underlying need to compensate for their shortcomings. Simply put, they feel better if they can cause someone else to feel worse. A lack of interpersonal sensitivity is a prerequisite personality trait.

flame war. When two or more individuals begin exchanging flames, or insults, online.

Shrinking the Narcissist's Mind

A **narcissist** is someone who is overly impressed with himself. He views other people as potential admirers as opposed to equals. An inflated sense of self-esteem causes him to believe

narcissist. An individual who cruises the net looking for attention from others.

that others are inferior. A narcissist also has a big appetite for attention. Narcissists on the Internet have a special challenge to feed that appetite.

Cyberspace, being the equalizer that it is, places all who enter on the same level. You can't show up in fancy clothes or cars. The house you live in doesn't matter. Who cares if you're sitting in front of the PC with a Rolex or a Timex? The customary social trappings that a narcissist uses to impress others don't work in **Cyberia.** So what's a narcissist to do?

> **Cyberia.** A synonym for cyberspace.

The usual strategy is to chat endlessly about oneself. A tendency to dominate the room or the conversation may be apparent. Another strategy is to play "cyber one-up-manship" in which everything you have and will achieve is better than the next guy. Of course if it's not real, it doesn't matter. Just make it up . . . who's going to know?

Shrinking the Sociopath's Mind

A **sociopath** is essentially an individual who has very little or no regard for others. He sees people as objects to be used in satisfying his needs, whatever they may be. Sociopaths are particularly hard to spot because they are manipulative and interpersonally adept. They're good at telling you what you want to hear.

> **sociopath.** A manipulative individual with little regard for others. The sociopath's sole purpose in being online is to use others to satisfy his needs only.

The Internet is an especially good medium for sociopaths because other users have fewer cues to go on. They can, and often do, take full advantage of the fact that the other person has little or no additional information available. The brighter the sociopath, the more difficult he is to spot. It wouldn't be far from the truth to say that the less intelligent sociopaths have brushes with the law, while no one catches the brighter ones.

The good news is that there isn't much of a hunting ground in cyberspace for a sociopath. At the same time they are out there, so be careful. The bad news is that the Internet can encourage an otherwise honest person to behave in sociopathic ways. It's so easy to misrepresent in cyberspace that an exaggeration can become a lie that builds into more lies and so on.

Shrinking the Dependent's Mind

A **dependent** personality type is someone who becomes overly attached to others. These individuals allow others to dominate them in exchange for a sense of emotional safety. In a sort of trade-off, they buy security at the expense of control. Low self-esteem and a lack of self-confidence compel the dependent person to create attachments that serve to compensate for perceived shortcomings.

dependent. An individual who becomes overly attached to others in cyberspace.

On the Internet, this translates into a tendency to rapidly establish multiple, close relationships. Dependents often follow exchanges of personal, intimate details with requests for phone calls, meetings, etc. They idealize these relationships.

cyberfriends.
Those online individuals to whom a user has formed emotional attachments.

Fantasy plays a large part in how dependent individuals view their **cyberfriends.** Usually, they see the other person as smarter, more accomplished and more capable.

The risk for the dependent person comes with the fact that a sense of rejection can easily arise in cyberspace. Let's see how.

Marie (Annie7) has met a number of friends online. Most of her social life has revolved around her favorite chat rooms and the regulars who hang out there. Recently, she met Mark (Quark) and they developed an online relationship that seemed to her to be close and intimate.

> *I really liked Mark. He was very bright and witty. We didn't chat all that much but I found myself thinking about him often. I realize that I get attached too quickly and easily, especially to men. I knew I was reading too much into it when after about a week of not being able to find him online, I took it personally. I thought he was more interested than he was. In retrospect, we had only casually chatted a few times but I still felt rejected. Why wouldn't he at least say good-bye?*

Mark was surprised to learn of Marie's reaction.

> *I chatted with her only a few times really. We talked about careers, hobbies . . . that kind of thing. I do that with a lot of people. I stopped using the Internet when I got assigned to a project overseas. I'm sorry she took it personally. Besides, I view it more as an entertainment medium rather than as a serious way to meet people.*

Marie experienced one of the risks of Internet relationships. They can disappear into the vastness of cyberspace at any time. Anyone can suffer the disappointment and perhaps hurt of losing what seemed to be a meaningful relationship. Dependent individuals are especially vulnerable, however, as they often emotionally risk too much too fast.

Shrinking the Cybersocialite's Mind

In any social gathering, some people are much more outgoing than others. These individuals seem to float around the room with ease and exude an air of self-confidence. They can interact with all types of personalities and are skilled hosts and hostesses. Fear of social rejection doesn't seem to be a concern.

In Cyberia, one can easily identify these **cybersocialites** by their friendliness and warmth. They are usually the first to greet a newcomer to the get-together. They're also more likely to be Cybercheers regulars who hang out in the same room or rooms day after day. Often, they will be there for hours on end and serve as social anchors for the rest of the visitors.

Cybersocialites may have a few different motivations for their gregariousness. For one thing, they may simply be sociable types, people who genuinely enjoy others and their company. They take

cybersocialites. Social leaders incyberspace. They often act as hosts in chat rooms.

pleasure in getting to know all the new and interesting people that are cruising cyberspace.

Another motivation is that many cybersocialites enjoy controlling the social flow of the room and dominating the conversation. An underlying need for attention and popularity drives these individuals to be highly social. A quick greeting at the door of Cybercheers by them is as much a statement of social dominance as it can be friendliness. It's like saying "Welcome to *my* party . . . glad you could make it!"

There's nothing particularly wrong about this kind of behavior. It can be very helpful. A cybersocialite often keeps the activity going and encourages socialization among quieter types. It's also comforting to many that when they show up at a particular room, there's often someone who's familiar there to say hi!

Shrinking Your Own Personality

The personalities of most cybernauts don't fit neatly into the categories just described. The uniqueness of each individual resists simple interpretation and generalizations. Yet, there are some questions you can ask yourself that will help you understand your personality in cyberspace and how it may affect others.

Q: What am I looking for in cyberspace?

A: Evaluate your motives for cruising the rooms. Are you looking for friendship, romance or sex? Are you just having fun, with no goal in mind? Motive dictates all behavior. So, consider what you are searching for.

Q: Am I basically honest with others?

A: Are your dealings with other people both on and off the Net basically honest? Sensitivity and respect for others will translate into truthful relationships where selfish needs take a back seat.

Q: Do I tend to be more assertive, aggressive or passive in my relationships with others?

A: *Aggressive* behavior reflects a lack of consideration for others, while *passive* behavior reflects a lack of consideration for oneself. *Assertive* behavior strikes a proper balance between others' needs and your own. Which style describes yours? The Internet can be a great place to try out assertive skills, especially in expressing opinions that you might otherwise keep to yourself.

Q: How big is my ego anyway?

A: Do you have a healthy self-image characterized by self-confidence and pride balanced with an appreciation for others? Is your ego so large it barely fits into cyberspace? Does your ego need some help to grow to a normal size? Whatever the case, Cyberia permits one to explore relationships in new and creative ways. Think of your ego as the rudder that steers your way through these relationships.

Q: How inhibited am I?

A: How inhibited or uninhibited are you? Is it your nature to be conservative and somewhat constricted or are you liberal and perhaps a little wild? The Internet will allow you to experiment with your less inhibited side in relative safety. Perhaps you'd even like to play with an alter ego for a while. It doesn't matter. Whatever you decide, there's plenty of room in cyberspace to let loose.

Remember that your personality is the outward manifestation of your thoughts, beliefs, attitudes and feelings. Other people see this reflected in your behavior and by what you communicate. What you say in Cyberia is often all that others have to go on in forming an impression of who you are. Be yourself, but be mindful that you're not alone out there.

SHARON'S STORY (Continued)

My husband wasn't really "into" what I wanted, but to his credit, he didn't see anything wrong or sick about it all.

I had seen Pieter in this room (#spanking) quite a bit. He was there under an assumed identity (which I didn't know at the time). He was there as a woman, Sylvia. He and his female business partner had begun this charade for several reasons. Before long, Pieter had made friends as Sylvia. He was very concerned about revealing his true self for fear of losing those friends.

He totally ignored me. I had watched him interact with others, and they seemed to respect Sylvia a great deal. I felt strongly compelled to make friends with Sylvia, though I didn't really have a rational reason *why* I needed her friendship. He rebuffed my every attempt to get to know him. This left me frustrated and verging on annoyed. I was a nice person, a good person. I made friends easily. Couldn't he see that? Nothing I did seemed to help. I finally complained to another channel member about Sylvia's coldness towards me. The man I complained to turned out to be Sylvia's best friend. He told me to just keep trying. He said Sylvia was a good person, and very nice, but she was European and maybe the language barrier was keeping her at a distance.

The same man who had praised Sylvia to me then went to Pieter and told him pretty much the same thing about me. He said that I was a

SHARON'S STORY (Continued)

nice person and worth getting to know. This broke the ice, and Sylvia began to talk to me. She and I would share coffee in the mornings together. Sylvia told me that she was IRCing from work. We became friends very quickly, and I felt a real connection to her, which confused me a little. We would sit in a private room, just the two of us, and talk for hours.

A few days after we met, Sylvia said, "I want to tell you something." I was open to hearing anything, so I told her to go ahead and tell me whatever she wanted. Sylvia said, "I'm afraid that when I tell you what I need to tell you, you'll run from me and not want my friendship anymore." This really touched me. I told her that her fears were silly, that I could handle anything she had to say to me and still care for her without any bad feelings at all. After a long pause, Sylvia said "I'm not a woman. I'm a man. My real name is Pieter."

This confession stunned me. This was *not* what I was expecting, and it confused me further. My first thoughts were that Sylvia/Pieter was a transsexual (an idea that now causes me to laugh) and that he had been hiding this from everyone. Sylvia told me that she was married, so my immediate response was, "Does your spouse know?" I can only imagine that he must have laughed at this and he asked me, (rather indignantly), "Does she know what???"

This began a long dialog about how he had gotten trapped in the persona of Sylvia and

SHARON'S STORY *(Continued)*

how he was fearful of losing friends because of it. He explained that he had told me right away because he felt we might become close friends and he didn't want another false relationship. He felt that I could handle his revelation and still care for him. Of course, he was right. I think that was the day I fell in love with him. It had taken real courage to tell me. His fears were too *human* and made him so vulnerable that I felt love for him right away.

3

Gender Gap on the Net

Subject: Genderspeak
From: Marky15

Why is it that men are forced to take all the risk in their relationships with women? We seem to assume the emotional risk when we ask her out with the possibility of being rejected. We assume the financial risk when we spend lots of money on fancy dinners and weekend activities, hoping to meet her expectations of what a successful man is. We assume the physical risk when we run to defend her honor with other men who have insulted her. Women's roles are changing rapidly in our society. They seem to be fighting for equality and respect and more options in life. Why can't women step forward and assume greater responsibility and risk in their relationships with men?

Subject: Genderspeak
From: GracyBee

What planet are you living on Marky15? I'm not sure what crowd of women you hang out with, but the women I know ask men out, buy them dinner, know how to use a door handle and rarely, if ever, need a man to defend her. It sounds like you have not availed yourself to the modern-day woman. Go shop elsewhere. There are many women out there who are taking plenty of risks in their relationships with men. Perhaps you have also missed the rise of the Career Mother, an unenviable role that leaves very little for oneself.

Subject: Why men just don't get it
From: Jean333

Men just don't seem to get it. They don't understand that by pushing themselves as power brokers, controllers of women, children and each other will not help them satisfy their need for love and appreciation.

In fact, as society changes, it will not support their goals of being successful in business at the expense of family life. There will be less tolerance for their self-centeredness and their need to dictate, direct and give orders. No longer will women accept the nasty, brutish quality of life that men seem to promote.

Macho control and sexist, racist, or any kind of exclusionist, POWER TRIP, ego-based behavior and thinking doesn't work in the long term any more.

That, in a nutshell, is what we mean by "men just don't get it."

Subject: Why men just don't get it
From: Glowstud

I'll tell you: As soon as men start "getting it," women will change it.

When you enter the world of cyberspace, it is interesting to observe the interactions taking place between men and women. The anonymity of online communication seems to be somewhat of a green light for people being more upfront with their thoughts, opinions and feelings. This new social arena is more tolerant of playful bantering between the sexes. What is so fascinating is that the battle field is equally advantageous to both men and women. Without having to confront the physical inequalities between men and women, the gender war in this virtual social arena becomes purely mental. Some of the exchanges between men and women are quite intense. After all, there are no moderators in cyberspace. Men and women more freely challenge each other without fear of serious consequence. Perhaps the open forum of gender-related expression will expand the minds of both parties involved, thereby narrowing the gap between the sexes.

Let's begin with the issue of what men and women are searching for when they enter the **cybersocial arena.** Men, it seems, are looking for entertainment and a place to unwind. They enjoy casual chat with others and are often searching for brief interpersonal encounters, often of a sexual nature. Women, on the other hand, are generally looking for meaningful connections. Their interactions are more personal and the intent is to develop ongoing relationships. In cyberspace, men click into chat rooms looking for entertainment and a place to explore fantasies. Although women enjoy the fantasy aspect of chat rooms, many are searching for lasting connections.

cybersocial arena. The plane in cyberspace in which various relationships between people take place.

Let's further examine this sentiment. The social arena of the Internet has become a place for men to escape the daily demands of work and family life. What do men typically do to escape from stress? They engage in some form of activity or entertainment (e.g., watching football, meeting friends out for a beer) as a temporary departure from their problems. Online we see this approach as well. Men perceive the cybersocial arena as a playground of sorts, a place where they can interact with great freedom and little accountability, a place to run away from the daily demands of work and family. Every day, the playmates change and new, brief relationships develop.

The Internet is also a place for women to escape the daily demands of parenting, work and marriage. However, women tend to rid themselves of stress in a very different way, making their approach to online chat different from men. When women's lives emotionally overload them, they seek out comfort from a friend. They want to talk about their problems and share with someone. Chat rooms, **newsgroups** and **bulletin board systems (BBSs)** are appealing to women in that they provide instant access to a community of friends who are there to lend an ear. Women, it seems, spend time online in search of meaningful communication. Bonding with others is the goal. Their chat often reflects real-life issues and feelings about things that are happening in their lives. For women, this virtual world becomes more of a quilting bee, a place to socialize and exchange stories. The

---

newsgroups. Usenet conferences that are organized by topic. Users are free to post messages related to the topics.

bulletin board systems (BBSs). A central computer you can connect to via your modem that allows the user to post messages, chat, send e-mail, and download files, programs and other information.

READER/CUSTOMER CARE SURVEY

If you are enjoying this book, please help us serve you better and meet your changing needs by taking a few minutes to complete this survey. Please fold it & drop it in the mail.

Name: _____

Address: _____

_____

Tel. # _____

As a special **"Thank You"** we'll send you exciting news about interesting books and a valuable Gift Cerfificate.
It's Our Pleasure to Serve You!

(1) Gender: 1) ____ Female 2) ____ Male

(2) Age:
1) ____ 18-25 4) ____ 46-55
2) ____ 26-35 5) ____ 56-65
3) ____ 36-45 6) ____ 65+

(3) Marital status:
1) ____ Married 3) ____ Single 5) ____ Widowed
2) ____ Divorced 4) ____ Partner

(4) Is this book:
1) ____ Purchased for self?
2) ____ Purchased for others?
3) ____ Received as gift?

(5) How did you find out about this book?

1) ____ Catalog 2) ____ Store Display
Newspaper
3) ____ Best Seller List
4) ____ Article/Book Review
5) ____ Advertisement
Magazine
6) ____ Feature Article
7) ____ Book Review
8) ____ Advertisement
9) ____ Word of Mouth
A) ____ T.V./Talk Show (Specify) _____
B) ____ Radio/Talk Show (Specify) _____
C) ____ Professional Referral _____
D) ____ Other (Specify) _____

Which Health Communications book are you currently reading? _____

(6) What subject areas do you enjoy reading most? (Rank in order of enjoyment)

1) ____ Women's Issues/Relationships
2) ____ Business Self Help
3) ____ Soul/Spirituality/Inspiration
4) ____ Recovery
5) ____ New Age/Altern. Healing
6) ____ Aging
7) ____ Parenting
8) ____ Diet/Nutrition/Exercise/Health

(14) What do you look for when choosing a personal growth book?
(Rank in order of importance)

1) ____ Subject
2) ____ Title Cover Design
3) ____ Author
4) ____ Price
5) ____ In Store Location

(19) When do you buy books?
(Rank in order of importance)

1) ____ Christmas
2) ____ Valentine's Day
3) ____ Birthday
4) ____ Mother's Day
5) ____ Other (Specify _____

(23) Where do you buy your books?
(Rank in order of frequency of purchases)

1) ____ Bookstore
2) ____ Price Club
3) ____ Department Store
4) ____ Supermarket/Drug Store
5) ____ Health Food Store
6) ____ Gift Store
7) ____ Book Club
8) ____ Mail Order
9) ____ T.V. Shopping
A) ____ Airport

Additional comments you would like to make to help us serve you better.

_____

_____

Thank You !!

FOLD HERE

BUSINESS REPLY MAIL
FIRST CLASS MAIL PERMIT NO 45 DEERFIELD BEACH, FL

POSTAGE WILL BE PAID BY ADDRESSEE

HEALTH COMMUNICATIONS
3201 SW 15TH STREET
DEERFIELD BEACH, FL 33442-9875

NO POSTAGE
NECESSARY
IF MAILED
IN THE
UNITED STATES

group participants remain relatively consistent. The mission is to develop lasting relationships.

In real life we all know that men and women are different in the ways they communicate. Generally speaking, men are great problem solvers. Their communication revolves around sharing information or facts that lead them to some type of solution. Men typically do not express feelings, but speak more on an intellectual or factual level. Women, conversely, speak more on an emotional level. Their goal is not to solve problems but to be understood. Women more often communicate about personal or emotional issues in hopes of having their feelings validated.

Online communication may afford men the first opportunity to share more on an emotional level. The anonymity of being online reduces the pressure for men to appear strong and in control. In our society men express their love and support by *working, providing* and *solving problems*. In cyberspace, men must learn how to connect with women via verbal expression. There is no opportunity to impress a woman by wining and dining her. A man must rely upon his verbal charm to win her. He cannot show her the things he uses to define himself. Instead, he must articulate his worth through the power of language. This is a challenge for men who have tended to be less emotionally expressive. However, it appears that men in cyberspace are quickly catching on.

Jay (Jaycee) from New Zealand had always had a difficult time opening up to women. He never knew quite what to say and often fumbled in conversation. Attracting women involved elegant dinners and rides in his expensive car. "My relationships never progressed much beyond the first date because I had little left to impress her with," he reported.

Jay got online through his business and entered the cybersocial arena. He initially struggled at the keyboard. Communicating online wasn't as easy as he expected, especially with women. Jay found himself discussing topics like politics, business and weather. It was difficult for him to hold a woman's attention for an extended period of time. Eventually, he tried a more personal approach. He shared his interest in various hobbies and talked about his relationship with an alcoholic father. He also made an effort to ask more personal questions of the women with whom he chatted. To his surprise, women seemed to connect with him in a different way. They shared more and were more interested in maintaining ongoing communication. Jay realized the value of sharing, allowing himself to be more vulnerable and talking about more personal issues. He commented, "There was a sense of safety in cyberspace. It seemed okay to talk about things that were personal. My connections with women online became more genuine than many of my real-life encounters."

Women online communicate personal feelings and issues. Many women are in search of being understood, and many are there to provide understanding. Women online are also in search of intelligent, stimulating conversation about current events, politics and business. Take the example of many stay-at-home moms who find online services to be a great diversion from the isolation and monotony of being full-time mothers.

Lesley (Legal1) had worked many years as an attorney before deciding to have children. It was difficult for her to find time to socialize outside her home responsibilities. She missed the interactions with her colleagues. "I felt like I was losing my identity. My only purpose was to meet the needs of my children. I felt alone and isolated from the intellectual world I once knew." Lesley's husband introduced her to online services as a means of connecting with others. He had been an avid online user for years. Lesley soon found herself immersed in chat-room discussions. With great ease, she could access hundreds of other stay-at-home mothers during the day. To her surprise she found that many other mothers were professional women who could relate to the changes and sacrifices of making the decision to be a full-time mother. The opportunity to meet many bright, interesting women online thrilled her. "I found myself discussing topics ranging from potty training to stock tips!"

While society often relies on women to keep the peace and expects them to keep their opinions silent, the world of cyberspace is providing them with a forum to express themselves with little risk. Women can say what they want as they sit safely behind their computer screens, often feeling liberated for the first time. Given the anonymity, the fear of retaliation or disapproval is of less concern. Women can more easily express negative feelings such as anger and frustration. Women find it much easier to communicate in a bold and assertive manner online. Let us not forget that in the real world it is still difficult for many women to assert their opinions and beliefs. Given the physical differences between men and women, there is still a tendency for women to feel intimidated and threatened in the presence of their male counterparts. Some women feel that the ability to communicate more openly online with less risk of retaliation encourages them to assert themselves more in the real world.

Men are also taking advantage of the anonymity of online communication. Like women, they seem to enjoy an opportunity to express their ideas openly without censure or criticism. Men appreciate having an open forum that allows them to express thoughts and fantasies that they often keep secret in real life. Here is an example of a posting that reflects the freedom one man feels in openly conveying his desires in cyberspace:

> *I am a married executive from Seattle. I need a female partner for sex and romance. I am willing to relocate the right person and will pay all expenses. I will offer a great salary if you are willing to do secretarial work in my office. Have to be attractive, in great shape and outgoing. You could*

be single or married. Anyone interested? E-mail me. Lovett632

Another interesting gender issue we observe online supports the notion that men tend to be more visually reliant than women. This theory becomes evident even in the world of cyberspace. In the absence of visual cues online, some men are quick to request physical descriptions of the person with whom they are chatting. Often women receive IMs from men asking for a physical description. Some men are especially visually reliant and ask for intimate descriptions such as, "What is your bra size?" This strong need for visual information may be the result of desires to fantasize about the woman. On the other hand, perhaps there is a need for men to find some way to "size up" their opponent. Women, conversely, seem more reliant on the content of their chats. They search for individuals with similar ideas and interests. They show less of an interest in knowing about an individual's physical appearance, and are more likely to ask personal questions to complete the gestalt.

Even the issue of sexual harassment is finding its place in cyberspace. There are plenty of jerks, both male and female, to meet along the way. We must all be prepared to face the challenge of online harassment. Men continue to outnumber women in the world of cyberspace, creating an atmosphere of male dominance. This atmosphere lends itself to crude comments and vulgarities.

However, more and more women are showing up online every day. There is no longer a sign on the clubhouse door reading Girls Not Allowed.

Approximately 33 percent of the 5.8 million people who access the Net nationally are women. Women are encouraging each other to be selective in where they choose to "hang out." For example, a chat room called Buxom Female Wanted would certainly pose more of a threat than a room called Woman's Point of View. Women online also support harassment-free zones. There is discussion about enforcing strict policies to create a safe atmosphere for women to interact hassle-free. On the other hand, many women admit the bold and often sexist comments from male counterparts don't bother them. Many of them view it as harmless fun. It allows them to banter back and forth without feeling intimidated by the presence of a man.

Although it is more often the case that men harass women online, women have harassed men as well. The crudeness and forwardness of women encountered in cyberspace often surprises men. Although some men enjoy a social arena that is tolerant of bantering between the sexes, others feel threatened by the outspokenness of women online. Here is a posting that addresses how some men react to the mere perception of the presence of assertive women online.

Subject: RE Gender Issues
From: Annabee

> *My husband went online using my screen name that happened to have part of my real name in it. He got into a discussion re: Bosnian Serbs about which he happens to feel passionate. He got so much flak from men who thought he was a woman, because of the strong opinions he voiced!!!! I had to laugh at the look on his face, and couldn't resist pointing out this is what women experience all the time. Strong women are such a threat!!! What a pity we all can't voice our thoughts without censure.*

Sexual expression online also seems to highlight a difference between the sexes in the world of cyberspace. Generally speaking, men are more sexually expressive in cyberspace in comparison to women. Women often complain that clicking into a chat room is like walking into a room full of men standing with their pants down screaming, "Hey, look at mine!" Men do seem to engage in much dirty talk online, which is similar to adolescent forms of sexual gratification: "If I can't get it, the least I can do is talk about it." Cyberspace offers men a perfect arena in which to engage in sexual fantasy without the pressure of having to perform or please their partner. There is less concern about measuring up to certain standards that women have. Again, there is great appreciation for the lack of accountability of their behaviors. Men take full advantage of the ability to play. For the most part, they say what they please.

While women are not quite as sexually expressive online, they too are experiencing much greater sexual freedom in the world of cyberspace. Women are taking advantage of the anonymity of the cybersocial arena by exploring sexual fantasies that they would ordinarily keep private. In real life where society measures a woman's sexuality by her level of physical attractiveness, women's physical appearance often inhibits them. There is a tendency for women to become preoccupied with the shape and size of their body, making it difficult at times to relax and enjoy sex. Online, physical appearance or attractiveness need not concern women. Physically, there is freedom to create whatever image they want to project. Engaging in sexual play online removes the barrier of body comfort. Imagination becomes the only limitation. As a result, many women express feeling less inhibited online, allowing them to explore various aspects of their sexuality for the first time.

At age 30, Holly (Neednfun) struggled with bulimia. She was all too familiar with the feelings of disgust she experienced every time she looked in the mirror. Her body had become her enemy. Real-life relationships with men were nonexistent. She couldn't bear the thought of being physically intimate and letting someone else see the part of her she had come to loathe. "Because I was so ashamed of my body, I assumed it would never be possible for me to experience a complete romantic relationship."

Holly's online relationships grew to be a source of comfort. She especially liked Ron (LABanker) who seemed so understanding and accepting. Holly's ability to flirt with Ron surprised her. One day he asked her to "go private." Holly knew what was coming, and she had to keep reminding herself, "He can't really see me." As Ron began exploring different parts of her "virtual body," she found herself passionately typing at the keyboard and sharing fantasies she had never shared before. "It was great not having to worry about being fat and unattractive. When I'm online, I can finally let go of the constant preoccupation with my body that haunts me day after day." Over time her online relationship with Ron became more sexual and intimate. "I'm not sure where this relationship will take me, but at least I feel safe sharing sexual intimacy with Ron."

Online users have said that the most thrilling aspect of online communication is the experience of being whomever you want to be. Online communication offers the opportunity to try on various hats. Many individuals go online impersonating the opposite sex. Perhaps this cross-gender role-playing can help bridge the gap between men and women. Many people report that by going online disguised as the opposite sex, they have developed a greater sensitivity to gender-related issues. By engaging in cross-gender role-playing, men have an opportunity to take part in more emotional exchanges without the fear of being perceived as weak or effeminate.

Women, on the other hand, can take advantage of the chance to be sexually expressive. Cross-gender role-playing allows women to explore sexual fantasies without being perceived as loose or aggressive.

Some individuals take the cross-gender role-playing farther than they expected, participating in sexual experiences they would never imagine in real life. Some people perceive this as harmless fun. Cross-gender role-playing does offer one an opportunity to get in touch with many aspects of one's sexual being. Where else can you get in touch with your most primitive sexual instincts without serious repercussions? However, no one should participate in sexual behaviors that feel uncomfortable or threatening.

Sometimes the thought of individuals disguising themselves as the opposite sex incenses others. One woman reported that a male co-worker engaged in a three-month online romance that abruptly ended when he discovered that "she" was a "he." She wrote, "Hell hath no fury like a man who has been deceived online by a man disguised as a woman!"

In the world of cyberspace the issue of gender seems in some ways more intriguing and powerful than in real life. Your experience online will be different depending on which gender you choose to project. We suggest that you take advantage of the anonymity of cyberspace and try some cross-gender role-playing. The experience will certainly bring to life some of the ideas we have discussed here. Perhaps you'll find that your entire online existence is more pleasurable when taking on the persona of the opposite sex! At the very least, we hope this disembodied medium will heighten your awareness of the gap that continues to separate men and women.

SHARON'S STORY *(Continued)*

My love for Pieter, in the beginning, was innocent and childishly simplistic. I honestly believed that it was just the love one friend feels for another. Maybe at that point it still was. When I told him how I felt about him, that I loved but only as a friend, he became nervous and almost embarrassed. He said that Americans threw that word "love" around too easily and without really meaning it. He said it was nice if I wanted to feel that, as long as I didn't expect the same from him. I smiled to myself and told him that my love for him wasn't dependent upon him returning the affection, that it simply existed and he would just have to get used to it. I would like to think he smiled a little every time I said to him, "I love you, Pieter, you're a wonderful friend," even though he would usually launch into his admonishment of me feeling too much too soon.

Pieter has a very tough exterior, and only a few people know that underneath he is a sweetly romantic dreamer. It is a side of himself he protects fiercely, but one that has endeared him to me. After a few weeks of only speaking through IRC and e-mail (both forums that are strictly textual) we felt the need to know each other better, and decided we should speak on the phone. Initially, Pieter was hesitant. He thought his voice would be displeasing and his speech too slow and lazy (qualities that I love in his voice). I convinced him that I didn't care what he sounded like and, finally, one afternoon he called me. . . .

4

Alt.Ego

Most people represent themselves honestly online, but cyberspace does create an opportunity for individuals to develop **alter egos (alt.ego)** whom they then present to others. An alter ego is essentially a misrepresentation of actual factual personal data or personality characteristics. Virtually everyone who has spent any time in a public or private chat room has talked to someone who is presenting an alter ego online. You may be one of these individuals yourself. Some cybernauts even have more than one alter ego depending on their mood or intention. These alter egos are often just slight variations or exaggerations of actual characteristics. However, they may also be complete fabrications, and of different sexes than the "real" individuals.

So, what is it about the Internet that allows these alter egos to exist? The answer to that question involves a deeper understanding of the marriage between technology and basic human nature. Let's take a closer look.

First, think of the Internet as "the great equalizer." Everybody enters cyberspace on the same

alter ego or **alt.ego.** A misrepresentation of actual factual personal data or personality characteristics.

footing. Individuals participate in various chat rooms based upon topic and interests as opposed to anything else such as gender, race, age, income level or religious group. It doesn't matter if you're the President or a civil service clerk. All cybernauts are created equal. Even rooms organized around what seems like an exclusive theme, such as Christian Chat, cannot deny participation by any one individual. There's no bouncer at the door of Cybercheers. Just pick a screen name and, *voila,* you're in. Sly Stallone isn't going to get into cyberspace's Hard Rock Cafe any faster than you are. Try doing that in New York.

Then there's the limitation of text. Unless you're trading GIFs, the only way of evaluating another individual in Cybercheers is through information provided by text. In the world of the Internet, you are what you compose. As the author of your own story, it's easy to give birth to an alter ego that in many cases is bursting to get out. If you always wanted to express yourself like Madonna, go for it. Who's going to stop you and who's going to know? If you can prove your case in words, that's about all it takes.

Let's see how easy it is to misrepresent yourself in cyberspace. Imagine that Tim (AKA) meets Tanya (NYC2) for the first time on the Internet in a room, Hopelessly Romantic. They spend a few minutes chatting and Tanya asks Tim to tell her a little bit about himself. Here are two versions of how Tim might respond.

Version 1:

> *NYC2: Tell me a little about you.*
>
> *AKA: OK. I'm 35, single, airplane pilot, 6 feet tall, 185 pounds, brown hair. Love fine wine, old movies, great conversation and . . . most importantly . . . the art and magic of romance.*

or Version 2:

> *NYC2: Tell me a little about you.*
>
> *AKA: OK. I'm 35, married but bored and looking, 5 feet, 4 inches tall, 216 pounds, brown hair. I work in car sales, have two kids and love sports, good beer and women . . . oops, just spilled some beer on my T-shirt!*

Which story do you think is more likely to make for interesting reading and keep Tanya online? You get the picture. If Tanya was in Republican Chat discussing politics, she might not care at all. It depends on where you're surfing and why. Motivation dictates direction. It's not that there is anything wrong with who Tim really is in real life. He may be a great guy. It's just that he wants to project a certain image to gain the interest of women. Seduction lives on the Net in all of its forms and alter egos make the seduction so much easier, as many people learn the hard way.

The primary reason that so many individuals create one or more alter egos on the Net is simple: They can. The Internet is the perfect technological medium that allows expression of anything you want in almost complete anonymity. Think of it this way. Imagine that Cybercheers is a type of stage in cyberspace where you can enter the room as any character you want. Want to be a woman but in reality you're a man? No problem. Tired of your career as a stockbroker? Be a sportscaster. Are you 52 years old but would like to be younger? Join 20+ Something and find out what the Generation Xers are thinking. The imagination is free to run wild on the Net and it very often does.

While the stage of the Internet makes it easy to be an impersonator, it also makes it the perfect setup for someone to fool you. Text-based interactions on the Net take place without normal sensory cues. As human beings we depend upon these cues to "size up" another person. There are no visual, olfactory, tactile or auditory channels to help us. We are missing essential pieces of information that our ancestors used to quickly determine if someone was friend or foe. In a real sense then, human interactions on the Internet take place in the context of "sensory deprivation." We can get away with being sensory deprived because we're so adaptable and have a wonderful ability to imagine.

At the same time, our minds form an impression. The human mind completes the whole image by "filling in the gaps" and creating a whole person. The image created will be a function of the information the sender communicated. Send accurate information and we're more likely to create a close approximation. Send bogus information and we get someone's alter ego. Remember that the image will also be the result of what we project onto the other person. This projection process also depends on our personalities, beliefs and attitudes towards other individuals. Information is open to interpretation by the human mind.

The majority of Internet relationships never progress beyond the screen. In these cases, alter egos usually go undetected. However, some do move from online to phone contact. Often, these relationships result in real-world meetings at some point. Each progression from Internet chatting to phone contact to real-world meeting adds new information. We then enhance the image in a positive or negative direction. Naturally, the more alter the alter ego, the more disappointment—and often anger—we experience. We like to get what's advertised.

The Net makes it easy to misadvertise. There is a tendency on the Net to present positive attributes and use the medium as a way to hide flaws—either real or imagined. Lack of information on the Internet can effectively cover insecurities that would be apparent in a real-life encounter. Hiding an insecurity, however, is different from projecting an illusion. In a real sense, of course, having an Internet alter ego can be a polite way of saying you're lying. Anyone who has spent any time on the Net knows that dishonesty can be a problem.

Is there any harm in all of this? For the most part, alter egos are harmless in chat rooms. However, they can be problematic when a relationship develops between two individuals and one of them violates the trust they share. The differences between how partners appear in cyberspace and how they appear in the real world surprise and disillusion many individuals who enter into intimate relationships on the Net. The extent of emotional involvement determines the degree of disappointment. Sometimes the creator of the alter ego finds that he or she has created a picture that they regret having painted. Let's look at Tom's story.

> *I feel so bad about not being nice to someone that I decided to write you and tell the story of what happened to me on the Internet. I hope that when people read this story, they will think twice before they do what I did. I am a male college student. I have my own computer connected to the Internet. As the only owner and root, I can assign any usernames, any accounts and create non-existing people on my computer. Once I created a female, Shelley (nice name isn't it?), and entered her into an IRC. Being a nice "girl," I chatted with quite a few guys, mostly to have fun.*
>
> *I was nice to them, smart and not very shy. People liked me, especially one guy. He talked privately to me on IRC and asked for my e-mail address. Yes, I gave it to him (on my computer . . . remember? I can create any account with full e-mail, information, etc.). Since then, he has sent me zillions of e-mails telling me how much he likes me and how he wants to call me, meet me, etc. I feel bad about him sending Shelley all these e-mails . . . but I don't want to admit that Shelley doesn't exist in real life.*

So, how do you guard against being misled? The consensus is that users should approach online relationships slowly. Getting to know someone over time will reduce the chances of being misled or hurt by an alter ego on whom you hadn't bargained. Still, as in the real world, there are no guarantees.

The question though is why would anyone project an alter ego out there anyway? A major motivation for developing an alter ego is that we all have sides to our personalities that we rarely, if ever, express because of fear or lack of opportunity. The Internet eliminates both obstacles. Using a cyberspace name and having seemingly endless rooms and bulletin board postings from which to choose, an individual can play in safety. The other inhabitants of cyberspace know as much about your real life as you care to reveal. You have control over your anonymity and power over who finds out what. That's nearly impossible to duplicate in real life. In Cyberia, you don't have to wear any social masks. On the other hand, if you wish to, you can try on different masks. A Net alter ego is usually an expression of a wish to be that person presented, if only for a short time.

Cybernauts who exaggerate real-life characteristics or develop full blown Net alter egos invariably enhance their image in a positive direction. They wish to appear younger, more attractive, thinner, richer and more interesting than they are likely to be in real life. After all, who wants to appear worse? Slight exaggerations are for the most part harmless and many individuals do tend to enhance their image now and again. For example, say you are newly interested in skiing and would like to converse with fellow enthusiasts. You're a beginner in a room full of ski bums. Someone in the room casually asks your level and you respond a little impulsively by typing in "advanced intermediate" or "expert." It's not true, but who's going to know?

The problem comes in when the alter ego persona gets much more attention and interest from others than the person's real-life presentation would. This can directly or subtly affect self-esteem as it confirms a person's belief that they are less interesting to others by being themselves. Anyone familiar with the story "The Secret Life of Walter Mitty" will appreciate this situation. On a positive note, rewarding relationship experiences on the Internet may transfer to an individual's real world as he or she develops more confidence in self-expression and self-acceptance. Success with an alter ego on the Internet may encourage an individual to try things out in real life. Check out Brigette's story.

Brigette (Brie) began Netsurfing about a year after a very painful divorce ended her 17-year marriage. Verbal abuse marked her marital relationship. Her husband would tell her she was unattractive, stupid and boring. Her self-esteem was at an all-time low and she was suffering from depression. Despite encouragement from friends, dating didn't interest her. She hadn't been out with another man in over 20 years and felt very awkward about it. She didn't want to go out but thought she might try some chat rooms at a friend's suggestion. Brigette enjoyed the camaraderie in certain rooms and (in a bold stroke for her) joined Flirts Nook one evening. The confidence and creativity of the participants, especially the other women, impressed her. Over the months, Brigette developed a flirtatious style that surprised herself.

> *My online personality was definitely an alter ego. I'd die if I was like that in real life. Anybody who knows me will tell you that. Wanna know who would hug the wall at a get-together? Me! Now it's different. I date and am finally working on undoing all the brainwashing I had. Men do find me attractive and interesting. My connections with my friends on the Net showed me that I could handle myself. It was very difficult trying it out in the real world at first, but now I feel much more confident. The Net gave me an opportunity to experiment in safety.*

While most users present alter egos deliberately, they can also develop unintentionally. A slight exaggeration here and there can build into more and more misrepresentations. As others become familiar with an online persona, that persona takes on characteristics that the person cannot easily reverse, except by changing screen identities. Once an "expert skier," always an "expert skier." If you are a "beginner skier" in the same room tomorrow night, you run the risk of others in the room embarrassing you by calling attention to your "demotion." Now that you really know how to ski, you may as well have been to Aspen and St. Moritz even if you've only glided down the bunny slope in Buffalo, New York. It's that easy.

In this sense, the world of Internet relationships can be a seductive medium. You can virtually connect with others in any way you can imagine so long as you have a willing individual or group on the other end. In the history of communication, it has never been so easy to impersonate yourself or others. The only limit is your creativity.

People have a tendency to be much more free-spirited on the Net than in real life. In a very real sense, the screen is your canvas and your words are the brush. What you choose to paint for others to see is up to you. When they enter the door at Cybercheers, everyone is an artist. Just remember that while many of the artists are realists, there are also many abstract painters. The catch is that it's hard to tell the difference.

Alter egos can also develop out of a need to express some facet of an individual that is normally controlled or hidden. Conflict takes place when internal desires collide with outside pressures. The more powerful the internal desire, the more conflict the person experiences if circumstances do not permit expression. Fear of punishment and social rejection often leads to inhibition.

Tom (BYO) is a married father of two who has never had a homosexual encounter in his life. He has, however, always had a secret curiosity about it. He has never told anyone, not even his wife. His alter ego BYO has had several erotic interchanges with other men on the Net.

> *I've always been with women and found sex with them enjoyable. Yet, I had a curiosity about other men for as long as I can remember. I even got close to experimenting with it in college but backed out because I thought it was "wrong." I grew up very conservatively and the guilt would have killed me. I'm more open-minded now, but still would never act out on it for many reasons. Still, I found that this desire was strong at times and I wanted some way to satisfy my interest. I remember I was scared one night but entered a gay chat room where I met someone who lived 3,000 miles away. He was also married and curious. We exchanged erotic fantasies and it was fun. It's enough for me. I'd never go beyond the keyboard. Every once in awhile I decide to explore this private part of who I am and feel safe in doing it.*

There's a very good chance that Tom would never have expressed this part of himself in the real world. Whether an Internet fantasy leads to action in the real world depends on the individual. Tom may or may not have had a longstanding conflict regarding this aspect of his sexuality. What is clear is that the Internet provides him with an outlet that is safer than others.

It's very important to understand this basic principle of human psychology as it applies to the Internet. Individuals will "approach" when they feel safe and secure, while they will "avoid" when they sense danger. Cyberspace is for the most part a safe zone in which to explore and play. It lets down normal psychological defenses and sets inhibitions free. There are fewer controls to modulate basic drives. In the language of Freud, the id gets more of a chance to play while the ego and superego stand by and watch. The world of Internet relations, especially postings in **usenet groups**, reflects a great deal of uninhibited thinking. In this sense, online relationships can serve a very useful purpose in allowing true self-expression. Cybercheers can be an outlet unlike any other.

Remember this: An alter ego on the net brings with it playfulness and a responsibility. On the other end is a human being whose thoughts and emotions you influence by what you say and do. In Cybercheers, as in real life, be kind and considerate of others.

usenet groups. A list of discussion groups on the Internet.

SHARON'S STORY (Continued)

Things moved very quickly after that first call. His wife had just gone to Croatia for a month and my husband was working out of state for many months at a time. Although Pieter should have been working (he and a friend own a consulting business), we began to spend hours and hours on the phone and on IRC. Our phone bills spiraled out of control and our work went to hell, but it didn't matter to us. We had found something in each other that was unique. Neither of us had ever had a friendship like this. We didn't care what it took to make it grow. We were willing to pay the price.

Finally, we had to admit to each other that we had fallen in love. This scared me and really sent me into a spin. I was an American housewife, for God's sake. I was meant for PTA meetings and limousine services for my child's after-school activities. The American housewife has a standard to uphold, a way to be that doesn't include such off-the-wall concepts as BDSM and falling in love with deep-voiced European relational database consultants. I measured myself by the sample put forth by my neighbors and came away lacking badly, but I was in love, and didn't have a clue where I was going with it.

Things were going just as badly for Pieter. He knew that when his wife came home and saw five-hour calls made every day to a phone number in the States she would go through the

SHARON'S STORY (Continued)

roof. His business was suffering terribly. He was leaving work early to get home to see me (by now his business partner had imposed a moratorium on IRCing from work), or not going to work at all for days at a time. We were, and felt, totally out of control. We wanted at first only to meet, face to face, to hold each other and make love and talk. Very quickly, though, we realized that we wanted something much deeper and more committed than that: We wanted to be married, to spend our lives together. This was pure torture, and though we found great joy in being together, life had become hell for us both.

5

Friends and Support Online

My name is Haley. I am a registered nurse with a Bachelor of Science degree in nursing. I am the nurse manager for a 45-bed pediatric unit at one of the largest hospitals in my area. Needless to say, I have a job with tremendous responsibility. Actually, I am just glad that I can go to work and function every day. Here is my story. . . .

Several members of my family sexually and emotionally abused me from—well the earliest memory to date is age 2—until I was about 13. These family members included my brother, cousins and uncles. In January of 1994, dealing with my abuse became too much for me. I sat with a gun in my hand prepared to take my life, but it didn't happen. A friend saved me. She found me a counselor who helped me stop feeling suicidal. I finally stopped all of my destructive behaviors, including cutting myself with razors. No, I was never hospitalized, which I am thankful for now. I know I was in real danger for a long time, and it would have been safer. I'm lucky to be alive telling you my story. I was in therapy for 10 months, and during that time I longed for, but could never find, the right support group for sexual abuse survivors. There were none in my area, but I continued to recover very well.

Then, in July of 1995, I began to have flashbacks of new abuse by an abuser I was not aware of: my father. It's still hard for me to think of him as my father, now knowing what he did to me. I have been "losing time" all my life, but it began to get worse. I began to come back from these times with cuts on my arms, and things being done that I couldn't explain such as writing, coloring, all kinds of things. I also became suicidal again. In September, I signed on to AOL and found the only support group of which I have ever been a part. We gathered in two rooms called Abuse Survivors and Abuse Survivors Lite. It is here that I met the only other sexual abuse survivors I know. This is still not a subject that gets discussed around the dinner table. Yes, I know there are survivors around me, but I don't discuss what I have been through any more than they discuss it with me. I began counseling again because my online friends encouraged me to get help. Now, my therapist and I are discovering that I actually suffer from multiple personality disorder. There are other parts of myself who have developed from a very early age in my life. These other personalities helped me cope with the abuse that I suffered.

Once my therapist and I identified my disorder, I began to pay more attention to when I "checked out." I examined my surroundings when I came back: Was the TV on now when it had been off before? Were things around the house in different places? All of this was at the suggestion of my therapist. I began to realize that my times "out" were times when things were going on, but I was not a part of those things. The confirmation came when Sara began to show up online. She is the six-year-old part of me. Sara started talking to my online friends, telling them that she watched when I talked with them. After my friends and I talked, we developed a plan that when Sara was online, they would log it and send it to me. I would, in turn, take these to my therapist, so that she could see what Sara was saying. It was all very scary for me. Actually, I was terrified. The thought of being out of control was very frightening to me. Now, Sara and I keep a notebook. I write to her and she writes to me. She colors, draws pictures, does all the things a six-year-old would do. We also have a contract: She is not to come out when I am working or when I am driving. She can come out at home only when we are alone. I used to have a screen name for her, but I recently canceled it in hopes that she would not go online anymore.

You see, Sara went online looking for help. She knew I was suicidal—that I wanted to be dead—and she was looking for someone to assure her that she would be okay. She was scared, and knew that my online friends would help me. She trusted them. Sara was online when things were bad for me, when I was cutting myself, when I was extremely depressed. My friends on AOL haven't heard from Sara for a while. Maybe she knows I am safe.

Online I have discovered a whole network of support. There is a place called Personal Empowerment Network and Issues in Mental Health. These places have support groups with facilitators. I also go into one called "Divided Minds" to meet with other multiples. In the online world I have found acceptance and safety, a place where I can discuss things when I need to. Most of all, I found a place where others understand me and accept me for who I am and for what I have suffered. There is no threat in cyberspace. If you were sitting here with me, I could never share my story. Because we cannot see each other, you cannot see the pain this has caused me. It is easier to tell you my story. I can be more honest, more open. I do not have to shield my feelings, as I have done all my life.

In cyberspace Haley was able to create a trusting environment. The computer became her friend. She exposed vulnerable parts of herself for the first time, and others greeted her with understanding and acceptance. Haley became part of a group that shared a common bond. The relationships were intimate, possibly unlike anything she had ever experienced in real life. With these relationships, she felt encouraged. She followed the advice of her online companions to get the professional help she desperately needed. In therapy, she discovered she had been suffering from the complexities of a multiple personality disorder. Her comfort in exploring these alternate parts of her identity in the safety of her online world seemed to facilitate some internal growth and healing.

Haley's story is one of many stories of individuals who go online seeking out friendship, support and a safe haven. Online relationships are becoming powerful forces in the lives of many people. The anonymity of online services allows individuals to share intimate parts of themselves. Sitting in front of the computer, it is easy to share personal tragedies as well as messages of hope and inspiration. There is always someone on the other end to empathize with your situation.

The exchanges of support and encouragement online provide an opportunity for many meaningful friendships to develop. In a world where we have become suspicious of our neighbors, politicians, teachers and religious leaders, it has become increasingly threatening for people to emotionally extend themselves. True friendships are hard to establish in the real world. Casual acquaintances are more common. In cyberspace, the anonymity reduces our fears and makes it easier to extend our hands to greet others. Because individuals are sharing such intimate thoughts, feelings and experiences, it is quite natural for friendships to form.

In early September, my 14-year-old daughter had an incident that appeared to be a seizure. Doctors treated her at the emergency room on Sunday morning. We set up an appointment with a pediatric neurologist for the following Wednesday. Sunday evening after putting her to bed, I sat at my computer screen, tired, scared and just looking for some mental diversion. I signed on to a general chat line and typed "Does anyone know anything about epilepsy?"

I received an immediate response from Carol in Oklahoma. She replied that the disease had afflicted her daughter, Lauren, now a college-educated mother of two, since age three. She suggested having her daughter join us online, too. I asked a million questions and they provided us with practical and informative answers.

The next few weeks, as we faced tests, specialists and uncertainty, this pair continued to guide me every day. They told me what to expect before every procedure. They spoke (online) to my daughter to reassure her, told funny stories about her daughter's adolescence and that this was in no way a death sentence. They prayed for us. I often wept in front of that blinking screen as the compassion of these two strangers enveloped me. Carol and Lauren became a part of our family. They were players in the dinner table conversation. As it became clearer that my daughter's case was not "text book" epilepsy, they cheered with us.

Even now that my daughter's health has stabilized, Carol and I e-mail each other and chat online nearly every day. We expanded from a crisis line to an over-the-fence relationship. We exchange recipes and Christmas gifts and philosophy. We talk on the phone and laugh over her Midwest and my New York accent. Online there are no accents, or any other things that will make you judge a person beyond their words. There is no question that this has helped make a huge difference in how our family reacted to this challenge.

Carol is coming to visit at Easter. I can't wait!

Ellen's story represents the strong bond of friendship that is common in the online community. She went online feeling confused and frightened. Another mother many miles away experienced the same fears about her own daughter's health. These two mothers joined forces, along with their children, to confront a challenging situation. In the end the news about Ellen's daughter was a relief. Yet even though Ellen's crisis was over, her friendship with Carol continued to grow. These two individuals had connected in a powerful way. Despite living in separate parts of the country, their lives remained easily linked by online communication.

These types of friendship stories are abundant online. Bonds of friendship are strong and meaningful in cyberspace. The social opportunities are endless and can be especially appealing to individuals who have a difficult time interacting in real life. Socialization problems are common to many individuals.

Remember the kids in your early school years whom everyone considered social outcasts: the kids who were always the target of taunting and teasing by their schoolmates, or the kids whom nobody ever picked for the kickball team? We all need acceptance by our peers, especially during our childhood years. Children need to feel that others support them and that they have friends. Unfortunately, many children become outcasts because of their appearance, a particular handicap or personality flaw. Each day of their social life reinforces feelings of low self-esteem and rejection. These issues carry over into their adult life where it becomes difficult to work, love and establish friendships. Many children and adults struggle with this painful issue and look to avoid social interaction at all cost.

The world of cyberspace can offer some of these individuals a chance to finally connect with their peers. Cyberspace becomes a place to try out social skills with little risk of rejection or ridicule. We can extend our hand, knowing there will be someone there to greet us. Here is Anna's story. It depicts the wonderful social opportunity awaiting individuals who feel isolated from their peers in real life.

Anna (Rosette098) was very shy as a child. She was born into a family plagued by alcoholism, and suffered neglect and verbal abuse as a child. Food became her source of comfort. By the time she was 5 years old, her peers already considered her fat. Other students taunted her throughout her school years and excluded her from most social activities. "It was difficult making friends. I had come to accept that people didn't care to be around me." Anna's social awkwardness embarrassed her parents. Her only comfort was another overweight child who understood the emotional pain of being fat.

In her adult years Anna's eating disorder was even more of a struggle. She had no close friends. Opportunities for interpersonal contact occurred only at her job. Employed as a nurse, she overheard one of her coworkers talking about online services. "I liked the idea of being able to communicate with people without the barrier of being overweight." She went online but initially found it difficult to participate in the chat rooms. One day she received an instant message from a man who was just "looking for someone with whom to chat." Their relationship developed quickly, and they found themselves chatting three to four times a week. Although Anna felt no romantic interest in this individual, she was greatly appreciative of the friendship that was developing. "I looked forward to my time online with Mark. He was so kind. Eventually, I got up the nerve to share my weight problem. The next thing I saw in front of the computer screen was: "LOL . . . ME TOO!" Mark encouraged her to become more active in various chat rooms, and even took time to introduce her to other online friends with whom he had become acquainted. In cyberspace, Anna finally developed the friendships for which she longed.

Geographic location, race or **SES** do not limit friendships in cyberspace. The enormity of online communication allows us to develop relationships with people very different from ourselves, making our lives richer and more exciting. Think of the intrigue of having a pen pal from a foreign place. The thought of hearing about someone else's lifestyle compared to your own is exciting and entertaining. Yet, the time involved in waiting for a response via snail-mail is frustrating. It takes years for pen pal relationships to solidify because of the time involved in communicating back and forth and the limited information exchanged with each letter. The idea of establishing pen pals in far away places loses its appeal because the gratification in connecting is not immediate.

Online services have now changed the way we socialize with people from different parts of the world. Now we have instant access to people from other countries. The immediacy of communication

SES. Stands for social economic strata, which is determined by factors such as income and profession. In cyberspace, all cybernauts are created equal . . . at least initially.

Netpals. Friends who connect online and continue their relationship through e-mail and other modes of Net communication. These are the online equivalent to snail-mail pen pals.

coupled with the low cost makes it easy to maintain these relationships over time. Here is Christine's story about **Netpals**, which demonstrates how strong the bonds of friendship become despite two people living in distant lands and never meeting face to face.

Last year I discovered that my university gave free Internet access to students. I took advantage of the opportunity to be online and began poking around on the Internet, trying to figure out how everything worked. One of the first newsgroups I stumbled upon was one dedicated to forming pen pal relationships. I answered a few, and got three responses. Two of them dropped off with time, but now, a year and a half later, I am good friends with my third pen pal.

This pen pal, or should I say Netpal, lives in Germany and is the same age as I am, give or take a few months. His name is Klaus. We started off just talking generally about countries and ways of life, but soon diverted from that. We write faithfully once or twice a week. Our sense of humor is similar. It didn't take long for us to become good friends.

During the summer, when I didn't have access to a computer, we kept in touch via snail-mail. Communication just wasn't the same. Nevertheless, we remained close. I found my correspondence with Klaus to be comforting. At our age (we are both 20 now), everything seems to change rapidly, and we need help adjusting. For example, Klaus was in the process of moving out on his own, to a completely different city, away from his entire family. I tried to help him with the anxiety that comes from separating from your family. Soon, Klaus will be starting the Germany equivalent of a university. I have been answering many questions about what he can expect, hoping that I have prepared him a bit. When Klaus moves, his computer will be practically the only thing that remains the same. He has asked me to stick with him through this transition. Of course I will be there because I have really started to care about him.

As for me, one of my brothers, with whom I am very close, is moving across the country in a couple of weeks. I don't feel ready for this adjustment, only being able to see him a couple times a year at weddings and funerals. Klaus understands this feeling because of his upcoming move. We shoulder each other's anxieties and make each other laugh. Just a few weeks ago I experienced a very significant tragedy. A close high school friend of mine died when she fell off a balcony. This happened days before term 2, and I found myself thinking that school seemed so unimportant, that we could all die tomorrow. Klaus helped me put things into perspective and basically get a grip. It was strange knowing that someone in such a far-away place cared.

The Netpal relationship established between Klaus and myself has become a treasured part of my life. He is my best friend. I share everything with him, even though I have never seen him face to face. We teach each other stuff, share much laughter and pain, and help pull each other through difficult times. It's comforting to know that as long as I have access to the Internet, I will never be alone. All I have to do is turn on the computer and my friend will be there.

This Netpal relationship became so valuable in the lives of two young people who came together to share their concerns and anxieties. The issues of death and individuation knew no cultural boundaries. At age 20, life felt complicated to Christine and Klaus. Online, they were able to share in the delicate transition from childhood to adulthood. They looked to each other to provide advice and support when confronting new challenges. Even though they had never met face to face, the strength in the relationship became a solid force in their lives.

For many individuals whom life has confronted with a challenging circumstance like illness, death or addiction, being online can be a place of comfort and solace. You don't need to wait for the next AA meeting or grief support group. Turn on your PC and access one of the many chat rooms or discussion groups that will offer you support and a wealth of information. Chat rooms have become a meeting place for individuals struggling with various problems. In many respects, chat rooms are similar to group therapy. Individuals come together to share life experiences and lend a helping hand. There is great comfort knowing you are not alone in your struggles. Hearing other members share similar conflicts and anxieties is a welcomed relief. Self-disclosure is more immediate, given the anonymity. Individuals share very vulnerable parts of themselves, parts they may have never shared before.

Theresa (LadyBlue) found a support chat room called CLADD (for Cleaning Ladies with Attention

Deficit Disorder). Diagnosed as a child with ADD, she continued to struggle as an adult with symptoms of decreased attention span and difficulty planning and organizing.

Theresa ventured into cyberspace and found the CLADD support group. Several of these women met online a few times a week to set goals that were difficult for them to accomplish in their daily life. After they stated their goal for the day (e.g., cleaning out a cluttered closet, paying bills, balancing checkbook) they would meet back online later to discuss how they did. Theresa found the group to be a great source for helping her cope with her ADD. "Other members encouraged me to follow through with tasks that I tended to ignore. Talking with other women who had similar problems was a tremendous relief," she expressed. The group members became part of her daily life. The individual stories of challenge and accomplishments kept her inspired and motivated her to overcome some of the problems associated with ADD.

From alt.support.abuse-partners (partners of sexual abuse survivors) to alt.support.youth.gay-lesbian (gay youths helping each other), newsgroups also play an important role in online support. This online medium is a place for people to tell stories of pain, growth and inspiration. Although less interactive than chat rooms, people still receive a tremendous amount of support and interpersonal contact. Newsgroups are especially useful as a means of imparting information. The subscribers become active participants and followers of the newsgroup and try to protect the group from unwanted intruders who have nothing useful to post. In many ways, newsgroups form very much like a family unit. There are experts involved who parent the group, providing useful information and suggestions to many of the participants. There are followers—or children—of the group who seek out information, support and guidance. It is surprising to see the level of human compassion and wealth of information shared in this online medium. In this forum people receive a great deal by giving and sharing.

> *I learned about newsgroups when I was working at a major university. During the summer of 1994 I finally got to access the Internet via our office computer. I was in a long-distance relationship with a guy in Lexington, Kentucky at the time and so the newsgroups that I looked into were about romance and long-distance relationships. I found one group called alt.support.loneliness that became my primary group.*
>
> *This group particularly became a great support for me when I moved to Lexington in September 1994 to be closer to my boyfriend. I started to find out in short order that the relationship wasn't as ideal as it had been from a distance. I was in much pain and I felt terribly lonely. Many people in this group seemed to understand the lonely feeling that I had even before this long-distance relationship began. We discussed how we all could relate to being in a crowded room, yet still feel alone. Many people offered explanations why we all might be*

feeling this way. Although there were many suggestions about how to change this part of our lives, we all recognized that it wasn't that easy to overcome years of social rejection, isolation and pain. Many of us had also experienced repeated failed relationships without ever being able to figure out why. I cherished the many thoughtful responses I would get each time I posted a note. I began to feel that the group was a place where I really felt understood. Perhaps for the first time in my life I could feel everyone pulling for me. The acknowledgment that I got from them was very reassuring to me in a time of great need.

When I moved to Kentucky to be closer to my boyfriend, he decided to back out of the relationship. You can only imagine how alone and abandoned I felt . . . no family, no friends. The feelings of isolation were unbearable. The group continued to be supportive. I really felt as if there was this little lifeline thrown out to me, and I clung tightly to it! The group was the only thing I had that was familiar from home.

What makes this story even better is that because of the group I met the man I married. Tom wasn't a frequent poster to the group, but he happened to be browsing one day. He somehow came across my poignant notes. He said that he couldn't help but write privately to me since I sounded so despairing, yet he recognized I was doing my best to cope with a bad situation. I was so grateful to Tom for extending such a broad shoulder on which I could cry. He wrote me some very accepting and supportive notes, never judgmental but always so insightful. His kindness amazed me. He kept writing back every time I sent him a long and redundant letter about my failing relationship.

Tom got me through an awful period of my life. His honesty allowed me to admit that I had made a big mistake in moving to pursue a relationship, not an easy thing for me to admit. After three months, I left Kentucky and moved to Virginia to be closer to one of my sons. It was a good move.

Tom and I continued to write to each other for another four months. There were no romantic feelings, or at least that's what I thought. Every now and then, I would think to myself that he seemed like the kind of man for whom I had been searching for a long time. My involvement in the alt.support.loneliness group continued. The members were happy that I had made a move, but I explained that I was still feeling very alone in life. Even with my son now closer, life didn't seem to have much purpose. The newsgroup continued to give me a sense of hope and encouragement.

In April I received a rather unexpected e-mail from Tom. He wanted me to consider coming to live with him in Canada. He explained that perhaps this would actually help both of us with our loneliness problem, despite the outcome of the relationship. After all, he felt that at least we would become best friends. Although this idea initially blew me out of the water, I found myself actually contemplating a move to Canada! Virginia had seemed like a new start for me, yet my loneliness continued to be a battle. I recognized that what I really wanted in my life was a lasting relationship with a man, and Tom seemed to be turning into that man.

Well, his proposal opened the floodgates in our communication. We started analyzing our relationship over the prior six months. Our first phone contact had been on Christmas Eve. Tom said he first started to care for me romantically after he heard my voice, how warm and caring I sounded. He didn't want to step in while I was in the midst of trying to sort out the other relationship. So, one thing led to another.

He sent me an airline ticket so I could fly to Canada to meet him in person. The big day came when I was able to embrace this human being with whom I had already felt such a closeness. It was like meeting an old friend. The attraction was instant. I knew immediately that I was falling in love with him. By the next day of our visit, we were talking marriage. There was some voice inside me saying that the time was right and the man was right, more right than I had ever felt before. We were married in June of 1995 in Virginia. Then we packed up my belongings and my teenage son and drove up to Canada. It has been seven months since that drive, and we couldn't be happier.

If anyone ever asks me if you can get support from online groups, I tell them a hearty yes! I got the best support partner for life.

Not only did Eileen discover tremendous support through her involvement in the newsgroup, she also found someone with whom she wanted to share her life. Her online world remained a constant at a time when her real world became less reliable. The familiarity of the newsgroup provided security. The members remained supportive and empathized with her feelings of isolation. Losing a relationship for which she had made a tremendous sacrifice was devastating. Eileen felt the members pulling for her, giving her the support she needed to move on with her life. The emotional strength among these individuals became her lifeline. What is even more heart-warming is that her postings captured the eye of a man who would make a permanent commitment to stand by her side.

Many of the newsgroups and various other discussion groups offer comfort and knowledge for individuals confronting various psychological conditions or problems. There are also a large number of support groups designed to assist individuals with various medical problems. These particular services offer tremendous emotional support and an opportunity to bond with others who are struggling with the same condition. Members share the latest medical information, talk about what to expect in various stages of treatment, offer advice to family members and provide a forum to vent the pain of coping with physical illness. Roger's story highlights the value of online interaction when confronted with a challenging medical problem.

> *A little over a year ago, doctors diagnosed me with Alpha1-Antitrypsin (AAT) deficiency. This accounted for the progressive shortness of breath I had been suffering for the last ten years or so. The doctor who told me I had emphysema was fairly stark in delivering the prognosis: "Think of it as a diagnosis like cancer," he said. I asked him about treatments and he told me that there were none, only transplantation when things became worse. Fifteen minutes later I sat in a state of shock in the hospital waiting room. I nursed a cup of coffee*

and wondered how I was going to break the news to my beloved wife of nearly 25 years.

I had never heard of Alpha1. This is hardly surprising as it remains a closed book to the majority of family doctors. Research in the U.S. shows that the average time between symptoms appearing and correct diagnosis is about ten years. The average patient sees seven doctors before one makes the correct diagnosis. Despite this, Alpha1 is the second most common genetic disorder in the U.K., after cystic fibrosis.

So, there I was, 47 years old with a lung function of around 50 percent. I knew that something had been wrong with me for years. Subconsciously I had already withdrawn from any physical activity and my wife nagged me about my lack of fitness. She tells me she thought I was just idle and how her view of me had tempered our relationship for years. She now feels deeply guilty about this.

In the days following diagnosis I became increasingly more anxious and depressed. I had to find out more about the disease than the scant information available in the local library. We did, however, find a reference to a U.S. support group and I wrote a letter and posted it as one might throw a message in a bottle into the sea.

Months passed and then a package turned up from Alpha National. This was a great help but still left so many questions unanswered. Having been into computers for many years, I decided to turn to the Net. I did find some medical abstracts on the **World Wide Web,** but could find no sign of any online support group. I posted a thread on alt.support.asthma entitled alpha1-antitrypsin and, behold, within hours a man who had contacts with some U.S. Alphas e-mailed me.

World Wide Web. A synonym for the Internet.

A contact: At last I spoke with someone else who was suffering the same disease. It is difficult to describe the feelings of relief I felt with that first contact. Until then, I felt tremendous bewilderment and isolation. During these initial contacts in September 1995, the slowness with which the answers appeared frustrated me. Always impatient, I would type my replies immediately, but have to wait days for responses. Then, someone put me in touch with another individual suffering from Alpha1. His name was André, and he lived in Montreal. He had a lung function of 22 percent. His younger brother had already received a single lung transplant. Over time I became very good friends with André, despite only "talking" via e-mails. He decided to set up a **list-serv** for Alphas. I had the privilege to be the first other Alpha to join. His international mailing list now has over 60 regular correspondents from countries including the U.S., U.K., Canada, the Netherlands, Australia, New Zealand and Sweden.

I cannot begin to tell you what a support this has been to me. I truly feel part of an international family. When I'm down, the messages of hope and encouragement help lift some of the darker thoughts. André is now working on a main WWW site for Alpha National and has designated a few of us as **Webmasters.**

My progressively poor health has led me to apply for early retirement from my lecturing post at a local college. If things go okay, then I hope to spend next winter in Florida with André, who "migrates" there each year to escape the rigors of the Canadian winter. It will be nice to be near someone who understands the challenge I must face.

list-serv.
An online mailing list.

Webmasters.
An individual responsible for developing and maintaining a homepage on the Internet.

Roger's story is not unique in that many individuals go online seeking understanding and answers in coping with medical challenges. What is unique about his story is that the medical community did not understand the illness that confronted him. The unfamiliarity of his condition heightened his fear and sense of despair. He truly felt alone and isolated. Online, Roger searched diligently for answers. His initial contact with another Alpha1 was his first ray of hope. Finally, he had established a link with someone who understood his suffering. This contact proved to be an important part of his healing and ability to move forward and confront a serious medical challenge. Connecting with other Alpha1s became his greatest source of inspiration and hope. His relationship with André became an important link in his life.

In cyberspace you will meet a plenitude of support and friendship stories that are truly heartwarming. People from all different backgrounds come together and exchange their stories. The intimate level of communication becomes fertile ground for the formation of strong interpersonal bonds. People remain more open in cyberspace, more willing to lend a hand to others in need. No matter how obscure your problems may seem, it is likely that you will run across some fellow cybernaut who truly understands your situation. For some individuals, cyberspace has become a place to re-establish belief in the compassion and benevolent spirit of humankind.

SHARON'S STORY (Continued)

I kept most of this from my husband, which was easy to do for a long time. He was in another state, so he didn't have to live with my obvious distraction and inability to get through a day without talking to Pieter at length. For Pieter, there was the sure knowledge that his wife would be coming home from her vacation with their son and that his emotional state was unstable. He would have to confront her with his feelings for me. He simply would not be able to hide them from her. I, of course, tried to talk him out of telling her about us, for purely selfish reasons: I knew she would be furious and forbid the relationship to continue. When it came right down to it, he had to do what was best for him, and I could not interfere. We tried to ignore the coming crisis and just enjoyed being together. By now, the facade of "Sylvia" had become very burdensome to Pieter. He was tired of pretending to be someone he wasn't. He wanted people to care for him for who he really was. He was also tired of hiding his feelings for me. When we were in public channels with many of our friends around, we had to behave as though we were only friends, and this was becoming impossible. People began to sense that there was something going on between us. People asked me privately if Sylvia was my lesbian lover. I laughed and told them to spread their gossip elsewhere. I think knowing that people were talking about me in this

SHARON'S STORY (Continued)

way—thinking I was a lesbian just because he was pretending to be a woman—may have bothered Pieter.

I had asked, gently, several times if maybe it wasn't time to kill Sylvia off and let everyone know who he was. This really worried Pieter, so I didn't push it. One evening, Pieter and I were alone in a locked chat room when I brought the subject up again. Maybe Sylvia deserved a decent death and burial. Maybe it was time. After much talk and hesitation, Pieter finally agreed.

6

Romancing the Net

In Cybercheers, the mystery and art of romance are having a field day. Thousands of people meet online every day, often by accident in a random electronic encounter. Some are looking for romance while others find it unexpectedly. Casual, public chat-room interactions lead to private chats and the exchange of increasingly personal information. Attractions develop and intrigue. Exchanges of e-mail are followed by phone calls, and then—for many—the first **IRL** meeting. This is the moment of truth when fantasy gives way to reality. First dates frequently take place after one or both individuals have traveled thousands of miles to meet. For some, the meetings are a disappointment. For many others, the meetings live up to—or exceed—expectations. Of these couples, some move in together and get married.

IRL. In real life.

So, where does all of this start? What is the genesis of so much human emotion over the Internet? It begins with a sense of safety, convenience and the written word.

Relationships have become more complicated than ever. The epidemic proliferation of sexually transmitted diseases in many ways makes the simple equation of "boy meets girl" an anachronism. Add to this the recent increased awareness of emotional and physical abuse in many relationships combined with concerns of date rape and a picture emerges that is complex indeed. These conditions are conducive to an atmosphere of mistrust and doubt. The basic drive to mate is often in direct conflict with the basic prime directive of self-preservation.

The Internet provides many with a *safe zone* in which people can meet and get to know each other in a more controlled fashion. The decision to become more involved tends to be more thoughtful for many cybernauts. If either partner is not prepared for the relationship to move forward, there is not as much pressure on them.

We've seen that the Internet is a medium that often encourages users to open up and become more personally involved than they might in a real-life setting. Sharing of intimate thoughts and feelings is commonplace. Individuals lower defenses quickly because they feel safe and less vulnerable in cyberspace.

Because individuals feel more security on the Internet, they are not afraid to ask questions. People are often afraid or embarrassed to ask personal questions in real-life, face-to-face situations. The Net allows individuals an in-depth medium for question and answer sessions. It's much easier to ask a prospective lover about personal issues such as how sexually active they have been or if they are disease-free. Of course, there is a hitch. Some people misrepresent themselves or lie.

In addition, the progression from simple chatting to romantic involvement usually occurs after the couple has established an online friendship first. Many individuals report that their online romance was more meaningful because of this friendship aspect. Individuals will get to know each other before they ever meet in real life. Romance finds its roots in the safety and trust that are the necessary conditions for intimacy.

Then there is the aspect of convenience. Cyberspace is open 24 hours a day, 7 days a week, 365 days a year. There is no need to dress up and go out to meet a prospective lover. Are you uncomfortable with the bar scene? It doesn't matter. It's actually very easy to meet others online. There are countless chat rooms representing all kinds of interests and attracting all kinds of people. Interestingly, many online romances begin in rooms that do not even have any romantic theme. In addition, someone who bores you can't trap you in a conversation. While Internet romances give new meaning to the concept of a blind date, they don't stick you with one person for the whole evening.

Think the art of letter writing is dead? Spend some time in chat rooms on the Internet devoted to romantic themes to get a flavor of what's going on. The wealth of creativity is amazing. The public rooms are just the tip of the iceberg. The private chat rooms and e-mails are where the real romantic action is. One could fill several volumes of a series titled *The Bridges of Internet County* by downloading a single day's worth of romantic exchanges on the Net.

The text-driven nature of the Net has helped bring thought back to the timeless ritual of courting. When you write, you need to reflect and think. Mindless small talk has little place in the romantic corners of Cybercheers. Choose your words carefully in Cybercheers, because the text that travels over the Internet can carry great power. Meetings between individuals in cyberspace and what they communicated there have changed the courses of thousands of lives.

Romance is one of the most intimate connections that two human beings can have. Romance is mysterious, exciting and hard to fully explain. The Internet is a medium that can pique one's romantic interest in combination with a heightened sense of human curiosity.

What you will find in this chapter are stories that reflect some of the many facets of romance and love on the Internet. Some stories are disappointing. Some are incomplete. Others warm and inspire the heart. The power of love and romance needs no explanation, not even over the Net. The Internet has simply provided love and romance with another path to someone's heart.

Mutual Interests— Monica's Story

I wasn't looking for marriage or even romance when I found Andrew. It was actually quite by accident. He, on the other hand, was in the market for a serious relationship, and had posted an ad on one of the BBW (Big Beautiful Women) home pages. I happened to remember some years ago a periodical called BBW Express, where men who appreciate large women (and large women who are looking for said men) place ads in this magazine. The editorial staff at the magazine sorts through the responses, and eliminates the raunchy ones, etc. I had seen this periodical and even developed a few snail-mail relationships that way. None which amounted to anything, but nonetheless I thought it was a good forum.

Through the Internet, I had already sought out (and found) Single Mothers By Choice, an organization I knew existed but which had eluded me for several years. I have a son who will be seven in August, and I am indeed a single mother by choice. I was pleased that they had their own home page, and I joined, hoping to make friends and find companionship through other women around the country who had made the same decision I had. Somewhere in my mid-30s I knew I would never marry, but did not wish to live my life without children. So this seemed the logical choice.

I was at the computer one day at the beginning of March 1996, grazing through the Net, when another possible "connection" occurred to me, my old friend BBW. I found all sorts of home pages, support groups, etc. It took some time, but once on a particular forum, it didn't take long to find

Andrew. The title on the section, Admirers, was Opera Goer. Oh my God! A man who appreciates large women and enjoys opera . . . this must be a dream! I am a classically trained musician and for the past five years have lived in a very small town where the musical possibilities, or even the hope of finding people with similar interests, are slim. Once again, the Internet was going to help me find a way back into the world I once knew and could relate to . . .

I clicked on his picture and found a short bio. Everything about this man appealed to me, so having his e-mail address in hand, I decided to send him off a short note. It didn't take long for Andrew to write me back.

In rereading our correspondence over the first three days, it seems we both became rather obsessed very quickly. We had similar senses of humor, and had a great deal of respect for each other. Although 3,000 miles apart, we started making plans to meet in July during my scheduled vacation in Lake Tahoe. Before we knew it, our phone calls increased, and our desire to meet grew stronger. Within a month, Andrew made the trip out here and it was love at first sight. Actually, we knew how we spiritually felt about each other through our correspondence and phone calls, it was just the anticipation of actually seeing each other and being together that was so scary. We seemed to get over that very quickly. Through our correspondence and phone calls, we had a pretty good idea how we would respond to one another. Neither one of us are introverted, and the computers were steaming a few times during our courtship One always prays for privacy in these situations!

Andrew proposed that weekend. There didn't

seem to be any question that he would leave the east for the west coast, as I had the more lucrative job with the most benefits, a home and a son. His familial ties were more limited, and he lived in an economically more depressed area. We made a few more visits to each other before we decided to get married over the Memorial Day weekend in Lake Tahoe. Andrew flew out again and we eloped on Friday, May 24, 1996. The following day we had a big barbeque for friends and family, and then announced our marriage. Needless to say, there was quite a bit of shock!

Andrew will be making the permanent move in early August (when certain job commitments have been kept), and both my son and I are looking forward to being a full-time family. The most important thing we have going for us is our firm commitment to make this marriage work, and there is no doubt in my mind it will. Believe it or not, there have been hurdles to overcome already, and we have accomplished them one at a time. Neither one of us has ever been married before, so there are additional challenges. We are both level-headed and communicate well, so combined with our senses of humor, we believe we can overcome all obstacles.

Most people don't understand how this nontraditional Internet thing could bring two people together so quickly. These are the people who have not used their imagination and follow traditional roles . . . these are sometimes the same people who live out their days alone. Marriage was never my goal, but it happened nonetheless. I have my computer, my imagination and my dear Andrew to thank for that.

BTW, my son is so very excited about finally having a dad! Andrew has accepted this role with *great dignity, and although a little frightening for him, is enjoying the challenge. It is interesting that I never knew how much Robert wanted or needed a father, being so wrapped up in the radical concept of being a single mother by choice. So we all learned a great deal from this.*

As Monica points out early in her story, she was not cruising cyberspace in search of a serious relationship. Andrew, on the other hand was looking for an online connection. His posting as an Opera Goer sparked her interest and the relationship progressed from there. Had he posted anything else, perhaps she would never have contacted him.

Her story gives the reader some idea about how meetings can take place over the Net. Many couples get together through chance encounters that one or both parties do not expect will be romantic. Sometimes these courtships move at very fast paces. They "met" in March of 1996 and were married by the end of May. While IRL relationships can move just as rapidly, Internet romances can often compress the getting-to-know someone phase. There's a tendency to get to the point more quickly in Cybercheers when it comes to establishing a serious relationship.

Monica acknowledges that over and above her love for Andrew, there will be special challenges to face. His move across the country, their new marriage and the change in family composition represent major life changes for all. Her realistic approach to those changes coupled with a philosophy of dealing with each challenge one at a time will help a great deal.

It's also important to note that Monica is very aware that her relationship with Andrew was based on an unconventional introduction. Her view is that love and meaningful relationships can be found anywhere there is an open mind.

Burning a Candle— Jason's Story

Within the last couple of weeks, I have met someone on the Internet via a CompuServe forum. When we first met in the forum, I was feeling very lonely and depressed. This person popped up and said hi, so I responded and we started chatting to each other. As we talked, it turned out that we had many things in common. She is 22 and I am 24. We found out that we both liked children. She is a professional nanny and I am a project manager for a company in London. We talked about everything—our likes and dislikes and what we both wanted from life. It really seemed as if we both wanted the same things.

Our first conversation went so well that we even exchanged telephone numbers and addresses. After our first meeting in the forum, we agreed to e-mail each other, sometimes two or three times a day. Every e-mail was just perfect and it really felt as if I had met the person of my dreams. After just four days, we started talking about the possibility of meeting each other. As I live just south of London and she lives in Cambridge, it was quite easy to do so I offered to drive to Cambridge to meet her. Right until we met, we kept telling each other how excited we both were about finally meeting each other, though we both also admitted to being a little nervous.

When we did finally meet, it really was a dream come true. Until that point, I had built up a mental picture of her and when I saw her, everything matched. Because we had been in contact with each other so much, it was as if we were already good friends and had known each other for a long time. We spent most of the day together at her parents' home. When her parents went out in the afternoon, we spent the rest of the day on the sofa just holding each other and showing the affection we felt for each other. The feeling was so wonderful and she remarked at how safe and secure she felt with me. I really felt that everything we'd talked about was beginning to come true, but I didn't really know at the time how she was feeling. From time to time, she would pause and look vacantly and I knew there was something on her mind.

We subsequently spent the evening together in her room and, for the most part, just held each other and kissed. She suggested that I spend the night also, and as the weather was very bad, I agreed. That evening, I stayed for dinner with her family and we spent the rest of the time together in her room. That night, she insisted that I sleep in her bed while she slept downstairs. She claimed that it would smell of me in the morning. We spent the night apart, though the next day she mentioned how lonely she had been, hinting that she'd wanted me to spend the night with her downstairs. As her parents were in the house, I didn't think this was a good idea. The next day, we spent more time together—this time closer than before.

Although we were both aroused, we did not make love. In the afternoon, while we were holding each other, she mentioned her ex-boyfriend. Up till now, she had kept it quite hidden, choosing not to talk about him for fear of hurting me. What she said really upset me and knocked me down as if someone had kicked my feet out from under me. She told me that she still had feelings for him. Although he treated her badly and even stole from her, she still felt feelings of love for him. As you can imagine, this shocked me because in her e-mail messages she had talked about how much she wanted to start over and meet someone new. I'm a very emotional person, so I began to cry a little. We held each other again and kissed a little and then we exchanged Christmas presents. It turns out that we both bought each other teddy bears. We kissed and held each other some more, but it was time for me to leave. It was sad as I hate saying good-bye, so we parted tearfully, my teddy bear sitting in the passenger seat of my car.

Since then, we have kept in touch but lately, things have begun to go wrong. I really believe that I am in love with Helen. I get all the tell-tale feelings—butterflies in the stomach, not being able to eat, etc. I told her several times how much I loved her when we were together, but not once did she say that she loved me. Even in our e-mails I mentioned that I was falling in love with her. I really believe this is possible, even though it was happening in exceptional circumstances. My feelings for her were real and still are. After this, I e-mailed her and told her how much I enjoyed meeting her and being with her, and how much I *loved her. However, she has told me that it will take her a long time to get over her ex-boyfriend and that she doesn't love me. Even the word "love" has disappeared from her messages. We had several arguments and she has made me say that I don't love her and that I was being stupid—fooled into thinking that I loved her.*

All along, I was only responding to what she had said she wanted and just being me. Like the romantic fool I am, I fell for it and really believed that things would work between us as we really seemed so perfect for each other. I was prepared to do absolutely anything to make it work and she knows that.

In the last couple of days, we have agreed to be just good friends, but I don't know what kind of friend she wants. I know I can't expect her to commit herself straight away, but the uncertainty is unbearable. During our argument on the phone, either one of us could have hung up as we both started talking determined to finish everything there and then. We hung on and talked for about an hour and in the end we agreed to be good friends, even laughing and joking—just as we used to in the beginning. I don't know where I stand. If I say anything, I feel as if I'm pressuring her and I don't want to do that. The problem is that she keeps her feelings hidden from me. All I know is that she wants us to be friends, but what for? For me to be used as I have been in the past? Does she want our friendship to develop? Does she see a chance for us in the future? I don't know . . .

Although I have agreed to be her friend, I know my true feelings and it is hard to keep them hidden, but I will do so rather than risk losing her completely.

Jason's story is a good example of a relationship that begins online with a strong fantasy component. He had a tendency to idealize Helen based upon their online conversations. While the relationship met many of his expectations, finding that his online romance ultimately turned out to be more one-sided than he expected disillusioned him.

It's likely that Helen was unaware that she still had such powerful unresolved feelings for her ex-boyfriend. The feelings that her meeting with Jason stimulated may have been as much a surprise to her as it was to Jason. The quickly developing cyber-romance with Jason may have been premature. It may have been a reaction to Helen's hurt following the loss of her previous boyfriend.

Helen's honesty with Jason about her feelings and need for time to get over her ex was painful for Jason to hear but necessary. Jason's hurt due to his belief that Helen misled him is understandable if that was the case. Allowing an Internet relationship to develop so quickly is emotionally risky as Jason found out the hard way. It's more prudent to move slowly in cyberspace as in the real world.

What will happen in the future, only time will tell.

Indecent Proposal— Karen's Story

I met an older man online. He told me he was 40, but I later found out he was 49. We talked for two months every night for sometimes hours.

Eventually, I started calling him at work. I would look forward to the night when he would be online, and I would put him in front of my other "real life" plans. I was going crazy. He was my knight in shining armor. He was a doctor and a scientist and a pilot, all professions that would attract any woman. I had such the perfect image of him. He told me that he had a hard life and so he never married and never had children. I thought that was odd for his age. I continued to question that, but he insisted it was the truth. I wouldn't have met him if he had an ex-wife or children. I'm much too young to get someone else's leftovers. Anyway, I eventually agreed to let him fly his plane in to pick me up for lunch. He was not handsome and was old. The reality of meeting him shattered my dream. I felt horrible guilt and disgust at myself for being so blind. That day he flew me to an island for lunch. He tried to be romantic, but I just wasn't into it. He was so intelligent though and I was extremely flattered that this man wanted me out of all the women in the world. You know, he was rich and successful, and I will admit, fun.

I saw him five or six other times. Once he kissed me, we became closer and he told me that he was in a bad marriage and still with her, and had two daughters, one of which was older than me!!! This hurt me and I felt so betrayed. Since that time, I have been able to remain somewhat of an acquaintance with him. He offered me $20,000 to sleep with him two weeks ago. Tempting as it was, I didn't do it. Then he said that if I would be his mistress, he would rent me an apartment near his house while I went to school.

The list of offered gifts goes on and on. This man drove me crazy, eventually to the point where

*I felt ugly inside. I still talk to him through e-mail and **IRC**. I don't know why I still do. I haven't seen him in four months and he always insinuates how sexy I am to him, etc. The flattery keeps me from telling him to go to hell, I think. It's sad to realize that about myself, but I am being honest.*

IRC. Internet Relay Chat.

Karen's experience demonstrates what can happen when false information leads an individual into a relationship that is very different from what it first appears. She found herself totally swept away by the false image her online partner projected to her. While he was not completely dishonest, he certainly left out certain important details. As Karen discovered, alter egos exist in cyberspace.

It seems from Karen's story that her self-esteem received a needed boost by this man. Her curiosity about why such a rich, successful man found her interesting reveals a deeper truth about Internet relationships. People go online searching for a relationship for different reasons. The power and status that this man represented attracted Karen. Her reluctance to break it off illustrates the fact that the relationship fulfills some needs. As her self-esteem improves, she is more likely to end her online relationship with this man.

I'm from Missouri: Show Me! —Mark's Story

I became involved in an online romance with a woman from Missouri. I live in Florida and accessed a BBS in Missouri. Dana and I started talking online and got along well. I had no idea that she had feelings for me. Her feelings developed before I even knew what was going on. Because the Internet is so anonymous, you can be anything you want to be.

She knew this and wanted to verify that I was who I said I was. Dana asked if she could call me one night. I agreed. She and I both knew that if I hesitated for any reason, the gig was up. We talked, and our conversation planted a seed in my mind. Over the course of the next five months, we talked on the phone countless hours, exchanged e-mail, hand-written mail, pictures, music, gifts, etc. We finally got to meet in person this past October. We spent a week together and our feelings are more intense today than ever before. Soon, I'll be starting a new job only two hours away from her and our life together will begin shortly.

Dana's request that Mark accept her phone call is a good initial test of trust when beginning an online relationship. Unlike Karen's experience in the previous story where her online lover had her call him at work, Dana was able to call Mark freely at home. A good question to ask oneself when beginning an online romance is, "Why wouldn't my partner talk to me at home?" There's certainly nothing wrong with being careful to whom you give your telephone number. However, as the online relationship progresses and becomes more intimate, a lover's reluctance to accept calls at home is something of which to be wary. Many online lovers are later disappointed, angry or hurt to find out their cyberspace partner is married or living with someone.

Mark's story typifies how many online romances progress quickly from chatting to full-blown relationships. Cyber-romances almost invariably involve a great deal of offline contact including phone calls, exchanges of pictures and so forth. They tend to be very intense.

The desire to meet face to face prompts the couple to arrange a trip so that they can finally connect. Dana and Mark's week-long visit met or exceeded their expectations and he decided to move to be closer to her. This is a common occurrence as many couples report that they felt when they finally met in real life, they already knew each other intimately.

Where There's a Modem . . . There's a Way—Britt's Story

*I don't really remember meeting Eric, my husband. I was hanging out on a (now long-gone) German channel and somehow we started talking. He had a **nick** that began with an H, and I was always confusing him with other Germans whose nicks began with the same letter. I only remember starting to think of him as an individual one day when we had a rather lengthy private chat, and at the end of it he told me, "You're really a nice person." At any rate, we were always happy to run into each other on IRC. He was a system administrator working for an options trading firm. Our time zones overlapped nicely because he would*

nick. Nickname.

stay up late; I worked different shifts, including early morning and overnight shifts as well.

In the summer of 1991, my company sent me to the Far East on a business trip. I took the opportunity to stop in Munich first to go to an IRC party. Eric knew I was going to be there, so he drove down, too (as he told me much later, just to meet me). We were staying with different people, but we spent some time together at the gathering itself. This included about an hour of him telling me everything he couldn't stand about Americans: They were all loud and obnoxious (he could spot one a mile away); they didn't speak any foreign languages (and he was telling me this in German!). As you can imagine, I would come to tease him about this later . . .

When I departed for Tokyo and Singapore, we kept in touch on IRC and exchanged e-mail whenever our schedules didn't match. I was now seven hours ahead of him instead of seven hours behind him. I even consulted him once as I was sitting in a machine room, working on a server that wouldn't come up, and asked him online for advice.

We shared our experiences by IRC and e-mail throughout the long winter: his car accident, his struggles with exams, the death of his grandmother, my stress at work. You can tell a relationship is becoming more meaningful on IRC when you start meeting on private channels rather than chatting privately on a public channel. It's more important to be with the other person than to talk to your friends, and you become afraid of accidentally sending something personal to the channel where other people could see it. We were geographically far away, but we always knew where the other person was, whether in the office, at home, on the way home, out shopping, or at a party. IRC lets you communicate minutiae in a way that e-mail doesn't allow in real-time.

Finally, my company sent me on another business trip, this time to Switzerland, close enough to Germany to make a trip worthwhile. I was almost afraid he wouldn't but Eric finally invited me to visit him at home. I would say it was after that visit that we were officially dating.

When distance separates you and you're dating by IRC, you have to make introductions where you can. I "met" his sister on IRC when she came to visit him; he let her log in and looked on as we chatted. On my first visit, he brought me to meet his parents, since we didn't know when I would be able to visit again. Some things in the relationship accelerate when you only see each other in person once in several months.

As time went on, we knew we were in love and wanted to be together; transatlantic trips were expensive and we couldn't afford them forever. We would spend all day on IRC, send e-mail besides, and then talk every other day on the phone. When you spend that many hours together, you run out of things to talk about, but you want to keep the contact, so you just keep sending the same silly phrases over and over again. We invented codes for "I miss you," "kisses," "someone is looking over my shoulder at the screen, so watch it," "still there?" "be right back—I gotta go to the bathroom," and more.

I was lucky enough to be able to arrange an expatriate assignment with my company to Switzerland. Eric drove down to meet me at the Zurich airport when I arrived there in August 1992, to start my three-year assignment. From that time on, we began to visit each other every *weekend. It was a four-and-a-half-hour commute each way by train, and we'd take turns visiting. The week was so stressful that usually I would get on a train Friday evening and arrive in Germany late at night. We would go pick up a pizza on the way home to Eric's apartment. We'd spend Saturday sleeping, and visit with friends or his parents on Sunday for lunch before I had to get back on the train and return home.*

Even though we were able to see each other on weekends, the commute was exhausting. We couldn't get anything done, and yet we didn't want to miss a single weekend. Spending all day on IRC and phoning every night still wasn't enough.

Eric resolved to apply for a job with another branch of my company, in Switzerland, about an hour's drive away, so that we could be closer. For months, we awaited the response to his application. There were days when it looked as though they would make him an offer, and other days when some facet of bureaucracy would rear up and get in the way. At the same time, it looked as though my company would cut short my assignment in Switzerland and they would bring me back to the United States. One day, a letter arrived out of the blue telling Eric, "We're sorry, we've selected someone else for the position," and we both broke down and cried. "Don't worry," I told him, "we'll be together, no matter what I have to do."

The day before Valentine's Day, 1993, we decided to get married. After a long paper war with the German authorities due to our different nationalities, we were able to get married on July 30, 1993, in the city hall of Eric's home town.

We still couldn't live together. Now that we were married, I had to apply for a permit for Eric to come to Switzerland. At the same time, he didn't want to move until he had a job there, and he couldn't get a job without a work permit. We continued to commute every weekend until January 1994, when he finally moved to Zurich to join me, just days short of our six-month anniversary.

Eric and I started out writing to each other in German on IRC; I don't think he would have taken the time to get to know me if I had written to him in English. In time, though, he switched from writing in German to writing in English, although we still speak only German at home. English has become our "online language," German our "real-life language."

Even though we now lead a more-or-less normal married life, we still spend time apart due to my business trips. When we can't be together, we talk on IRC and send e-mail. I recently spent three months in London where, yet again, we spent our weekends commuting to be together. Even as I write this, I'm sitting in London in our new apartment, while he sits in Zurich, watching the movers pack up our belongings so that he can join me.

The fact that Cybercheers is unrestricted by geographic location permits couples to connect from faraway places. Cyberspace eliminates the usual boundaries that separate people. As can be seen from Britt's story, she met Eric who was in Germany at the time while she was in the U.S. Their meeting was unplanned and the possibility of their ever having met initially in real life was a remote possibility at best.

Many individuals end up traveling thousands of miles to finally meet one another. It's quite common for couples to be from different countries. Of course, dating someone across the state or across the world brings with it special challenges and frustrations.

Britt's and Eric's courting and ultimately their marriage is an inspiring testimony to the power of a loving relationship. A casual online chat developed into a full-blown romance that prompted both of them to make major decisions to be together. Their commitment to each other overcame the geographic obstacles they faced, although that was a difficult process.

Many couples face the frustration that Britt and Eric experienced. Fortunately for them, they were able to work it out. Unfortunately for many others, the complications of maintaining a long-distance romance prove to be too much and the relationship stops or changes back into something more of a friendship. Each outcome is as different as the uniqueness of the couple themselves.

SHARON'S STORY *(Continued)*

We decided that we would go into #spanking, where all of our friends were sure to be on a Saturday night, he as Sylvia, and me as myself. We would mingle and chat with others for a bit, and then Pieter would change his nickname to a masculine name, and announce that he was a man. My hands were shaking badly, and I think his might have been too. We went into the channel, and sure enough all our friends were there, maybe 30 people in all. We chatted and said our hellos and then I said to Pieter, "Sylvia, it's time. Tell them." Everyone slowed their talking to listen, no doubt expecting us to announce our lesbian love affair, and wanting to hear all the dirt about it. I was terrified for Pieter, and thought that I had never seen courage like this before in my life. He waited for a moment and then he changed his nick to "Pieter." Before anyone could react, he knelt [users describe movement and actions in a style called an /**action**, and read something like this: "Pieter kneels before Sharon"]. "Sharon, I love you, and I want everyone to know it. Will you marry me?" I had not been expecting this at all, and I burst into tears, sitting there behind my screen, imagining him down on one knee, proposing. I was so overwhelmed and so proud of him and all I wanted at that moment was to be his wife. Not caring for the consequences, I accepted.

The chat room erupted. Everyone was babbling at once. Some of our closest friends were

SHARON'S STORY (Continued)

happy and congratulated us. Others were furious and hurt that Pieter had deceived them. I fielded private messages for the next 15 minutes. I wanted to talk to Pieter, but I knew others were inundating him with a flurry of messages. I suspected that many of them were not very nice. After a few minutes, he'd had all he could take and logged off suddenly, vanishing.

I was devastated. I felt as if this was my fault and that he was losing friends because I had asked him to kill off his persona. I felt selfish and sat there crying and telling people repeatedly, "Yes, he really is a man; no, it's really not a joke; PLEASE don't hate him, he needs your friendship." It was horrible. Finally, feeling like a little pebble against a sea of water, and imagining that it had been worse for Pieter, I logged off as well and sat and cried. I tried calling him a few times that night, but he wasn't answering the phone. All I could do was wait for him to log back on, and hope he would do it soon.

7

Affairs of the Net

Hate to blow the lid off this one, but there are many affairs going on in Cybercheers. They range from simple flirtations to graphic cybersexual flings. Chat rooms such as Married and Bored, Husband Is Outta Town and Married but Looking are often starting points for individuals interested in beginning a relationship online. Consider, for example, Ray's story. Ray, an investment banker living in the Midwest, met Lisa from Colorado in a popular chat room, Hot Tub. Ray liked her profile and their flirtations began innocently enough. Lisa was married, worked as an accountant and had two children. Ray was married with three children of his own. Ray thought some of her comments in Hot Tub were witty. He decided to send her a private message and they ended up spending about an hour chatting about careers, children and marriage. Towards the end of their chat, Ray decided to get a little bold and asked Lisa if she was happily married.

Ray: *Mind a couple of personal questions?*   :) Smile.
Lisa: *I'm game . . .*
Ray: *Are you happily married . . . :) . . . or not . . . :(*   :(Frown.

Lisa: Ladies first, huh? Not in this case! What about you?

Ray: OK then, . . . married but bored.

Lisa: Uh oh! You mean there's another married, bored person cruising cyberspace? lolol

Ray: Yeah, I think there are at least a couple more.

They agreed to "meet" in cyberspace at 11 P.M. the following evening. They spent three hours in a private room chatting about their personal lives and exchanged physical descriptions. Over the weeks, a relationship developed that included regular cybersexual encounters that were more than a little steamy. They would graphically describe their fantasies about each other in detail, often with their spouses in the very next room!

Ray: I've missed you . . . thought about that bottle of wine with you in the hot tub all day!

Lisa: Like that fantasy huh? . . . would you like it if I gently licked the wine off your fingertips while I slowwwwly . . . teasingly . . . pulled down your bathing suit???? Mmmmm????

Ray: Almost as much as I'd enjoy feeling your heart beat faster and faster as I caress your shoulders, run my fingers through your hair and passionately, deeply kiss you . . .

Lisa: You're making me HOT Ray!!!

Ray: Hope so!!!

Are Ray and Lisa having an affair, or is it simply a harmless fantasy that exists only in cyberspace?

The answer to that question will likely depend on whether you ask Ray and Lisa or you ask their spouses! Most cybernauts don't consider online affairs to be "real." After all, the relationship happens over a modem, not in a bar or motel. There are no glances, no touching, no exchanges of bodily fluids. Many times they've never even talked to each other. Most spouses, however, aren't going to see it the same way. Reactions from spouses who "catch" their partners playing in Cybercheers vary from individual to individual.

Melissa's husband, John, had been having a cyberfling with a woman for a few months when she "caught" him online in a compromising position.

> *John had always been into computers, so I was used to him spending hours on his PC. I noticed that he was up later and later at night cruising the Internet. One night, I found myself curious about what he was so into. I didn't intend to sneak up on him, but he didn't notice me come into the room. I glanced at the screen and was shocked to find him talking to some woman about how he'd like to throw her on the bed and make wild, passionate love to her. I was furious and hurt. We had quite a blow up about it. John accused me of overreacting and insisted it was harmless fun. I didn't get the joke and told him to cut the "relationship" off immediately.*

Susan's husband, Alex, spends a few hours a week surfing the various chat rooms, sometimes in search of an erotic encounter. She knows about

Alex's interests and it doesn't bother her because she feels it doesn't take place in the real world, only in cyberspace.

> *I don't really care if he's playing around online. We're both secure in our relationship and I see it as a harmless outlet as long as it stays on the computer. We have an agreement on that point. No exchange of identifying information and no phone calls.*

Susan is an exception. Melissa's response is more typical. Most partners regard this type of online interest as a threat to the relationship. In their view, having a fantasy is one thing, but sharing it over the Internet with a stranger is something altogether different. They have a point there. It's not as though people engaging in online flings are interacting with an anonymous series of computer links. They are involved in online relationships with other people who exist at the other end of the modem. Those people are often married themselves. Complicated, isn't it?

What is it about the Internet that makes having an affair so easy and why are people doing it? Let's consider the first question about the ease of having an affair in cyberspace. The Internet makes it effortless to meet other people. In many cases, it's much easier to meet someone in cyberspace than in real life. Taking risks on the Net is a no-brainer. If a contact doesn't work out, it's no big deal. Just move on to the next encounter. You can afford to be bold on the Net. You don't have to get up the nerve to go up to someone in Cybercheers. Just do it! Under the protection of your **cyberhandle**, everyone can have the confidence of Don Juan.

Also, relationships on the Internet often progress much faster than they would in real life. People ask personal questions more quickly and take more risks than in a face-to-face setting. The conditions are more conducive for an affair because people get to the point much faster. Couple that with the fact that the theme of a room is shorthand for what's going on in your life. You're probably not interested in discussing the intricacies of playing chess if you've clicked into Looking for an Affair. Kind of cuts to the chase, doesn't it?

It's also much easier to have a **cyberfling** if you consider cyberspace a virtual playground. As we've mentioned, most people don't consider affairs on the Net to be real. They think of them as entertainment and a way to play out fantasies in a safe environment. Cybercheers is "out there" somewhere in cyberspace, not "in here" in one's own home. They can flirt, seduce, tease and have safe sex with a partner they never talk to if they don't want. After all, how can you be cheating when your virtual "partner" is thousands of miles away and your own real-life spouse is asleep in the next room? As Anne (Veronica) likes to put it:

> *I admit that I like to flirt and occasionally play out sexual fantasies on the Net with select partners.*

cyberhandle. An individual's unique online name or nick that often communicates something about that person.

cyberfling. An online cybersexual interaction, usually of a casual nature.

But I draw the line by never going beyond the keyboard even though I've been asked to. I'm certainly not having an affair but I am having fun. When I turn off the PC at night, it's my husband's bed I climb into, not my partner in cyberspace. I'd hardly call that an affair.

Let's not forget the question of safety and discretion. After all, who's going to "see" you out and about? There are no relatives, friends or co-workers to worry about. In Cybercheers, it's pretty safe to play. At the same time, playing online doesn't come without its risks. As in real life, this can be part of the excitement. There will be more on that later.

Now, for the second part of the question: Why are people doing it? Why wouldn't some guy who's just spent two hours chatting with a woman 3,000 miles away, turn off his PC and talk to his wife? Why would a woman from Seattle climb into a cyber hot tub with 22 strangers, when she and her husband have one in their very own back yard? For much the same reason people gather at any club: the escape appeal and a reprieve from the demands and responsibilities of life, if only for a short period of time.

Better yet, why not escape to a fantasyland where you can play with an idealized partner? After all, the guy conversing with the woman 3,000 miles away is very unlikely to have any issues with her. She is whatever he imagines her to be, based upon what she's told him. She doesn't hassle him about watching sports, picking up after himself or anything at all. She talks sexy and thinks he's great. She's the perfect playmate. Why isn't his wife more like her?

He's pretty wonderful, too. He's polite, hangs on her every word and what a great communicator! On top of that, he's so romantic and a world-class lover. Why isn't her husband more like him? There you have it: an ideal partner with whom your imagination can run wild. What could be more exciting? The fantasy appeal of the Net is enormous, and we have an insatiable appetite for fantasy.

Besides enjoying the escape value, many participants see affairs of the Net as antidotes to boring marriages. If their real-world relationship has gotten stale, then a cyberaffair can serve as a way to alleviate that boredom. That's how Andrea (Foxy21) views it.

Andrea has been involved in a cyberaffair on the Internet for about a year now. She and Chris (F451) are both married with children. They "meet" regularly in Cybercheers for private chats at least four times a week. Andrea reports:

> Sometimes we just chat about things going on in our lives and other times we get more intimate and sexual. He's a great conversationalist and knows me very well. It's amazing, but he can read between the lines so to speak and can sense when I'm having a rough day. To be honest, my husband usually doesn't have a clue about how I feel and here's this guy over a thousand miles away who's

more in tune with me. My marriage is pretty routine and boring. Chris is exciting and interesting and I look forward to our "conversations."

Chris sees it much the same way.

Andrea is very bright, articulate and witty. I love stimulating conversation and she's interested in me. My marriage isn't too hot. Bland would be a good word for it. The sexual excitement is awesome with Andrea. We've had more intimate sharing of fantasies than I've ever had with a woman before, including my wife. If there's such a thing as safe sex in the 1990s, this is it!

Andrea's and Chris' story is typical of many thousands of online couples. Aside from dealing with boredom, their motivations for a fling on the Net illustrate another major reason why some people are having these types of affairs: They have deeper problems in their own primary relationships. These problems usually have to do with poor communication. That's ironic considering these cyberaffairs are so heavily reliant on clear communication. Other typical issues concern work pressures, financial worries, children and the usual litany of life's demands and responsibilities that can push people apart.

Where there's a problem, there's also a need to solve that problem. The basic appeal of Cybercheers is that it draws us to a place where others understand us. We also want intimacy. An affair of the Net is another way to achieve the intimacy that may be missing in a marriage. Intimacy, romance and sex are the spices of a relationship and very powerful psychological forces. We also need attention. If we're not getting it at home, for whatever reasons, we're more likely to seek it elsewhere. The Internet is a simple, convenient and relatively safe way to have these needs met.

If two people are sexually involved on the Net, then they may be having wilder, more passionate sex than either have had with their real partner, or ever in their lives for that matter. Let's not forget that the world's greatest sexual organ is the human mind. An affair often involves excitement from taking risks without anyone finding out. Just as in the real world, the appeal of doing something wild can be a turn-on, especially if the rest of your life is full of responsibilities and pressures. Joan (JoJo) finds the risk to be part of the appeal.

> *I've been "involved" with a man on the Internet for 6 months now. It's a very enjoyable relationship for me. Bob is bright and funny. We have frequent erotic encounters that are very explicit. Most of the time my husband's in the other room. Sometimes he's in the very same room. It's exciting thinking that I'm doing something this close to home and I could get "caught" any time. I really don't want a problem on my hands at home, but the truth is it's fun to be a little naughty now and again. I feel that it's okay because I'd never take it any further.*

We have found that it isn't uncommon for spouses to catch many of JoJo's cyberspace counterparts online, often in compromising positions. Sex in cyberspace may be far from equivalent to the real thing but it can be just as destructive to a marriage depending on the issues and personalities involved. Before you decide to play, you should consider the risks to your current relationship.

The fear of being found out has spawned a number of creative strategies designed to protect the affair in cyberspace. The easiest and most common strategy is to play while the partner is away. The whole idea of being "home alone" takes on a new meaning. The use of private passwords and multiple cyberspace names is also a frequently used method of protection. What if the partner is at home? Surely no one would be that risky, right? Wrong.

A user in Greece advises keeping the mouse arrow set on the minimize icon in case of "cyber interruptus." A veteran of cybersex from India recommends a strategically placed mirror to warn of approaching intrusions from a partner. Many users are surprised to find that their partners have been watching over their shoulder for quite some time. As you might imagine, a number of interesting discussions have started this way.

Do cyberflings undermine the marriage or provide the participant with a safe outlet for desires? Again, it depends on the personalities involved. Romantic or erotic interludes on the Internet can definitely lead to cutside involvement in the real world just as any other flirtation can. They also can and often do stop at the keyboard. As with all intimate connections, the personality and circumstances of the individuals involved will determine the direction the relationship will take. Cybercheers is a meeting ground. The members decide what's going to go on there.

Oh, What a Tangled Web We Weave—Kurt's Story

My Internet relationship began the last week of July 1995. It started out innocent enough, just talking about general things. One night I told her my real name was Kurt. I asked her if she could tell me her name. She said she normally wouldn't, but said it was Maria. I liked her, but did not think the relationship could really lead anywhere. I only had access to the Internet from work and I was off for the next four days.

I later found out that she logged in every day looking for me. When I logged back in four days later, she said she'd been looking for me and asked where I'd been.

A few nights later, after we'd exchanged e-mail and we were getting more personal, she asked if she could call me at work. I said sure and gave her the 800 number. We talked for about 10 minutes. I loved her voice. We began speaking on the phone any time we had the chance. One night online, she said "I love you Kurt." I wasn't sure how to respond. The next day, I was beside myself. I didn't know how to take it. I was falling in love with this woman and I had no idea what she looked like. The next night, I told her, "I think I'm falling in love with you." We both fell hard, fast and deep. I thought about her all the time. I'd come home from work and pace the floor wondering what the hell I was doing.

I had a wife of nearly six years, and a son under the age of two. I wondered if anything could come from it; should anything come from it. I was miserable when I couldn't talk to her and she felt the same way. I decided to see where this would take me and we exchanged cards, letters, pictures, music tapes, personal items. We had always talked about meeting in person, but I lived in California and she lived in New York. In September, I bought a plane ticket to go be with her.

Her husband was going to be out of town for the weekend and her two daughters, ages 14 and 16, were going to be at friends' houses. Before I left to go to the airport, my wife found my ticket. I had told her I was going to Chicago to spend the weekend with my mom. The ticket said New York, not Chicago. We had a fight that could have signaled the start of Armageddon.

That Friday, Maria said I needed to try to work things out with my wife because we were over. I slipped into a coma. I was miserable. I went home to my wife and agreed to try to work things out, but my heart wasn't in it. I could not stop thinking about Maria and how much I loved her. I cried when my wife wasn't watching me. I missed Maria. The next day my phone rang. Whoever called hung up on my wife when she answered. I knew it was Maria. Something inside told me it was her. I made up an excuse to go to the gas station and called her. She was just as miserable as I was and we agreed that we couldn't end it. We wanted and needed each other too much. We agreed to put it behind us and pick up where we'd left off.

Finally, after five long, painful months from the time we fell in love, we touched for the first time. I had feared that what we had online might not exist in real life, but I was happily mistaken. It was more wonderful than I could ever have imagined. We spent a week together in October.

Her husband still had no idea because she was with me during the day and after work only. That week, I decided to do whatever I had to do to be with her. Leaving her, even though I knew I'd be back, was excruciating. I got back and told my wife it was over: I wanted a divorce.

I began looking for a job in New York to be closer to Maria. On October 7, I got one. On October 14, I signed the divorce papers and on November 5, I left California and headed for New York once again—this time for good. Maria and I spent Friday evenings and Saturday mornings together. We went to the beach, stayed at my hotel and made love, talked, laughed, drove around and shopped. I adored spending time with her. For the first time in my life I was truly in love, and she felt likewise.

She wanted to wait until the end of the school year in June to tell her husband. However, this past Monday her husband's supposed best friend caught us walking on the beach. We had been kissing every 20 feet and doing other things. That night, she told her husband. It has now turned into exactly what I most feared: a decision for her.

I am not pulling her. I told her that I would not do that. I want what's best for her and for her to be happy. I know that if she stays, it will be for her kids. She will slowly die on the inside without me. I do believe in the idea of soulmates and I know now that's what we are. I don't want to influence her one way or the other. She is thinking of her kids and that's good, but she's excluding her feelings. She lived far too long an unhappy lie before she met me. I want what's best for her and if she decides to stay, I will wait for her. I know she will come back to me. I don't say that out of naiveté, but heartfelt fact.

Kurt's progressive involvement with Maria over the Internet is not an unusual occurrence. Their cyberaffair began casually, only to progress to the point of an actual IRL affair. They even admitted feeling love for each other without having spent any time in each other's presence. That will no doubt sound very strange to those uninitiated in the ways of the Internet. We're here to report that it happens all the time.

Kurt's observation that their affair began innocently enough is not entirely true. They may not have been overtly looking to contact a prospective lover in cyberspace but they certainly were unhappy in their marriages. The conditions were ripe for an affair. If either Maria or Kurt were happy in their relationships at home, it would never have happened.

It's not unusual for people to engage in affairs, fall in love and break off their primary relationship in favor of a partner who they believe will make them happier. What is unusual here is that the unique properties of the Internet put two people together from opposite ends of the country who otherwise never would have met. As their relationship moved forward and they supplemented telephone contact with exchanges of letters, cards, pictures and personal items, Kurt and Maria decided to take the risk and begin an IRL relationship.

Maria fulfilled Kurt's fantasy of her. This too is an experience that cybernauts often report. The friendship and intimacy that develops over the Internet are powerful emotional experiences for many. Kurt and Maria will have to see if the reality of a day-to-day relationship replaces their honeymoon period. As always, each couple is different. The complications of their involvement are still unresolved, and their ultimate future together is difficult to predict.

What is clear is that they should openly and directly address the conflicts in their respective marriages with the goal of either separating, divorcing or working on the marriage. Only in this way can they sort out the tangled web.

SHARON'S STORY (Continued)

The next day Pieter was back online. Amazingly enough, he seemed to have adjusted already to his new "self." He told me that he had felt overwhelmed by the uproar and had logged off in sheer unhappiness. He felt better now and was even more convinced that he had done the right thing. This greatly relieved me. After Pieter's "coming out," it became widely known in the Undernet BDSM chat community that we were now a "couple."

Our relationship, our feelings for each other and our need to be together escalated after that. Very soon, we had almost forgotten that there was anything else on the Internet but our hours and hours of talk and sharing. We isolated ourselves. He changed his nickname, as I did mine.

We were now, unofficially of course, "engaged" and one afternoon, after spending our usual hours and hours of talking and laughing together, Pieter asked me again to marry him, in real life. I could not . . . I have a viable marriage and a daughter who adores her father. Pieter knew this and insisted anyway and I suddenly decided that I would marry him. He would become my IRC "husband" and I would be his IRC "wife." I had no clue what this meant or would come to mean to us in the future.

SHARON'S STORY (Continued)

We called together some of our close friends, went into a private channel and "performed" an impromptu wedding ceremony, complete with wedding vows that came straight from our hearts, rings and champagne. It felt very surreal to me, and my head was swimming by the time it was finished. Pieter said things to me during the ceremony that wrung my heart and made me cry with love for him. I was suddenly "married" to two men, and although this was not a legal marriage, the commitment to each other was very real. I finally realized that I had to tell my husband all of it. I knew that when he came home from his extended business trip I would be unable to hide not only my feelings for Pieter, but also the phone bills I was stockpiling.

8

Cybersex, Cybersex, Cybersex

Online Host: *** You are in Hot Tub.***

Sxylags: HEY Y'ALL I'M HAVING A PARTY. DOES ANYONE WANT TO GO?

Blaze 232: Hello Sxylags!!!!

Kalvespt: Can I come with you?

Babe4u: Include me

Sxylags: TO THE HOT TUB WE GO!!!!!!!!!!!!!

BryDude: What's going on here?

Chiaras2: <————————-gettin' my fins

Steve KC: AM I INVITED TO THE TUB? CAN I MAKE THE BUBBLES?

Sxylags: ————————————————
>>>>>>>>taking clothes off, jumping in . . . close your eyes guys.

Blaze 232: Well all right, here I come. I am stripping right now!!

Babe4u: Everyone get their masks and snorkels!

BryDude: Can I help anyone get undressed?

AnnaSx: Taking off my clothes————————
————>>>>doing cannon balls in the hot tub

Sxylags: Where are all guys? Hot babes in hot tub . . . join us for fun!!!!

Kalvespt: <————————————————
————belly flop into the tub, move over ladies!

CalvinK: *Just walked in, parties {sic} in the tub<————————————here I come!!!*

Blaze 232: ————————————————
SPLASH! WATER FEELS GREAT.

Steve KC: *BOY there are some nice bubbles in the tub, just a rubbin' and a tubbin'.*

Sxylags: *Who needs baby oil . . . I'll do the rubbin' in the tubbin'.*

Chiaras2: *Wearing a sexy, string bikini guys . . . shall I take it off?*

BryDude: *. . . Take it offfffffffffffffffffffffff Chiaras.*

Kalvespt: *Rubbin' oil on Sxylags' back . . . he . . . he!!!!!!!!!!!*

Chiaras2: *(teeth chattering)*

Blaze 232: *Undressing Chiaras from behind while kissing her . . .*

SteveKC: *I'll get the VCR.*

Babe4u: *I need some lovin' in the tubbin' . . .*

Chiaras2: *Ohhhhhhhhhhhhhh . . . feels sooooooooooo good Blaze!!*

Sxylags: *<————————————————
—holding breath, going under . . .*

CalvinK: *Moving over by Babe4u . . . kissing her lips . . . rubbing oil on legs!!*

In cyberspace, sexual innuendoes are common and hot chatting is rampant. When it comes to requesting sex, people are far from shy. Many of the chat room names reflect the popularity of sex online (e.g., Short Skirts, Nude, Hot Hubby Home Alone, Married but Looking). It is difficult sometimes to know what you will be walking in on when you click into a room. You may even find yourself blushing a bit with the open, forward hot chatting that often takes place. Whatever your desires are, it is relatively easy to find a partner who will join in your sexual fantasies.

So, what do we see with this marriage between modern technology and sexuality? We see the transmission of sexual fantasies via the computer, which we have all come to know as cybersex. Many people have a difficult time understanding what cybersex is. Very simply, cybersex is the online equivalent of engaging in sexual acts in the real world. It involves two or more people typing their sexual fantasies back and forth with the purpose of mutual stimulation. While most people find satisfaction in sitting at their keyboards in a state of sustained sexual arousal (just short of orgasm), others find it necessary to remove their hands from the keyboard for a short period. Do you get the picture?

Unlike the real world where it usually takes days, weeks or months to cultivate a sexual relationship with someone, in cyberspace you can expect things to progress more rapidly. One minute you're simply flirting, "female, blue eyes, 28, love to take you for a ride in my Porsche," and the next thing you know you find yourself having steamy cybersex, "my lips are moving down to your . . ." The major difference is that people are making virtual love. Sex in cyberspace becomes a purely cognitive, creative and emotional exchange, rather than a physical one.

In a world plagued by sexually transmitted diseases it is easy to understand why cybersex is rampant and becoming the talk of the online town. The free love of the 1960s no longer exists in the real world. People are more sexually cautious than ever before. The days of hanging out in local bars with the intention of having some type of sexual encounter are less common. Unfortunately, the fear of communicable disease has in some ways spoiled the fantasy and fun of courtship and romance in our society. Online services have gained popularity at a time when society is looking for alternative, safer methods of sexual expression. Cybersex is just that: a physically safe alternative to real-life sexual encounters.

How do people come to engage in cybersex? In many ways cybersexual relationships develop just as they do in real life. People find themselves hanging out in chat rooms, searching for someone of interest. Yet, the absence of behavioral observation means finding someone who "sounds" sexually appealing or of interest. The Internet forces individuals to get to know each other from the inside out as opposed to from the outside in. Conversation that one finds stimulating and enticing heightens sexual interest. Verbal passion, not behavioral gestures, is the basis for seduction.

When you find someone interesting in the same chat room, you may eventually ask that individual to "go private." You are asking them to leave the bar, so to speak, and take a stroll outside to get better acquainted. "Going private" allows two or more people to engage in private conversation online without being "overheard" by everyone else. Private chats can lead anywhere, depending on how well the two individuals connect. For those hot on the trail for cybersex, private chats usually end with two people (or perhaps many more) hopping into a virtual bed. Think about it: There is no lag time between meeting someone and driving home to have sex.

Yes, many men and women are engaging in cybersex online, perhaps many more than would care to admit. The truth is that people feel less inhibited sitting behind their computers, and they are able to share intimate fantasies that are often difficult to share in real life. It's exciting to know what your partner is thinking during moments of intense passion. What feelings or fantasies navigate his or her every move? There's no need to worry about the way you look to your partner! The physical barriers we often find in the bedroom are not present in cyberspace.

Cybersex is generally more spontaneous and adventurous than real-life sex. Individuals come together and collaborate a rich sexual fantasy, delving into very private, erotic thoughts. Many individuals express sexual desires that they feel would be unacceptable to their real-life partner. The anonymity makes one feel less inhibited. There is little accountability with cybersexual encounters and most of these relationships are short-lived.

What makes cybersex so appealing to many online users? For some it's an opportunity to express sexual fantasies and desires that are too difficult to express in real life. Melissa's (Melrose) own sexual exploration online amazed her. As a young child, her stepfather molested her. The emotional scars of his abuse left her feeling sexually vulnerable as an adult. She had been married for many years and loved her husband deeply. Yet it was a challenge for her to let down her guard, even with the man that she loved. Melissa was reserved, frightened and unable to share her sexual fantasies. "When I made love to my husband, I found myself mentally leaving the bedroom. I felt so detached." She had never been able to share a true level of intimacy with her partner of 12 years. Friends had suggested she go online as a means of developing more support in her life. She became quite interactive in chat rooms, gravitating to private chats with individuals who felt safe and supportive.

In time, Melissa found herself sharing some of her sexual fantasies, fantasies that she had never been aware of before. "I enjoyed luring men into hot, passionate chat. I projected many personas. Some were reserved, others were pretty loose." This new sexual freedom soon carried over into her marital relationship. Melissa felt more sexually in tune when making love to her husband. Never before had she allowed her mind to work in unity with her body while being sexually intimate.

Being online broke down barriers in her sexuality, allowing her to connect with her husband in a more intimate way. Melissa expressed, "I never imagined that I could feel so close to another human being."

Many people also enjoy cybersex because of the lack of emotional commitment. **One-night cyberstands** are quite common and certainly more acceptable than in real life. If you don't like the way your partner fantasizes or you feel your partner is not creative enough, move on to the next cybersex lover. No strings attached.

Online, many people enjoy the freedom of sexual expression without all the responsibility that is a part of a committed relationship. This is especially true when the world overwhelms us with responsibilities and commitments as partners and parents. After all, society is now much more aware of what it takes to be an emotionally healthy individual and to maintain a healthy relationship. The media bombards us with messages in support of psychological well-being via taking responsibility for our lives and maintaining healthy interpersonal relationships. In the world of cyberspace, some of our needs for attention and sexual expression can be met without having all the responsibilities of a serious connection.

For many individuals, engaging in cybersex offers the freedom of sexual experimentation without serious risk. Cyberspace allows you to try out your sexual fantasies in a place free of sexual boundaries and limits. Unlike reading a

one-night cyberstand. A brief cybersexual encounter that does not result in the development of any kind of meaningful relationship online or offline.

self-help book on improving your sex life, cyberspace is a virtual reality playground in which to experiment and receive real feedback from your partner. You've heard many therapists say how important it is to talk about your sex life. The truth is that it's easier said than done. Online, the anonymity makes sex talk quite easy. Expressing your sexual desires and giving honest feedback to your partner becomes relatively painless. There is less concern about being embarrassed or sounding silly. When you take away the physical act of sex, as in cyberspace, it becomes a purely cognitive and emotional exchange. Cybersex usually lasts much longer than real-life sex, where it becomes easy to focus on the physical release only. The expressive foreplay in cybersex is endless. Typing out your fantasies forces you to be more sexually creative.

Jim, a single physician, lives in Oklahoma and cruises the Internet occasionally in search of a cybersexual fling. Cindy, an attorney, is also single and lives in Michigan. They met in a chat room six months ago and have never seen each other or even spoken on the phone. Occasionally, they connect online after a quick check reveals their mutual presence in cyberspace. They say hi and update each other on what's been happening in their lives. Both Jim and Cindy enjoy this foreplay. They know that in a little while one of them will break the ice and suggest something sexual. They've been to bed in cyberspace about 20 times and each time the scenario is different.

Jim: Cindy . . . you know what honey?

Cindy: What?

Jim: I have a rose for you . . . —{—(—(—@ . . . now, come close to the screen . . .

Cindy: Yes baby, I'm close . . . what is it?

Jim: Closer . . . I want to whisper this . . .

Cindy: I'm ready . . .

Jim: I want you, I need you, now sit back and imagine this . . . imagine me gently rubbing your neck and your shoulders . . . relaxing you . . . you notice the smell of your favorite cologne as you anticipate what will come later . . .

Cindy: Mmmmm . . . honey, tell me more . . . I do want you . . . gonna make me wait?

Jim: Waiting will make it better . . . I take you by the hand and have you lie on the bed . . . I want you to keep your clothes on as you watch me undress . . . slowly . . . first my shirt . . . exposing my chest . . . then my jeans . . . you like the way they hug my body so I turn around and pull them down revealing my black bikini underwear . . . I'm already aroused as I turn towards you . . .

Cindy: My turn baby . . . :) . . . I pull you down on the bed and you feel the curves of my breasts against your chest as I kiss you slowly, deeply exploring your tongue with mine . . . I now have you lie on your back and tell you to watch as I undress for you . . . I take off my black cocktail dress and you become even more excited as you can see I'm wearing a low-cut black bra with matching panties, a garter and stockings . . . I walk back over to the bed and pull your underwear off and begin to lick you . . . perfectly . . . just *the way you like it . . . when you're really good and aroused I tell you I want you now . . .*

Jim: *I kiss your neck and shoulders, then your breasts and begin to gently move my body into yours . . . you gasp as you feel me for the first time knowing we'll be making love for hours in all positions . . . my sole purpose is to drive you crazy . . . to be your best lover . . . I begin moving more rapidly . . . then slowly again teasing you, arousing you more . . . until I focus all of my erotic being into you and have you orgasm for the first time . . . the smile on your face tells me you're pleased and so am I . . . :)*

Cindy: *Now it's your turn baby . . .*

As you can imagine, Jim's and Cindy's erotic language is tame compared to what really goes on in many of these private chats. The power of language becomes ever so vivid in this cybersexual exchange. Take away the physical aspect of sex and it becomes an act of communication, two individuals sharing intimate wishes, desires and feelings. As you can see, cybersex is less one-sided than many real-life sexual relationships. After all, you can't just lie back and be a blank screen! Both individuals must participate to keep the fantasy alive.

If you were able to take a glimpse of private chats in cyberspace, they would amaze you with the sexual creativity that exists in the minds of online users. By exploring cybersex, you can add to your repertoire of fantasies and desires. You can also learn a great deal about being sensitive to the needs of your partner. Online lovers pay attention to their partners and how their partners respond to their fantasies. There is less room for pure self-gratification in the world of cyberspace. Individuals learn about their ability to be creative and attentive lovers. There is no need to worry about appearing awkward or clumsy. The worst that can happen is that you develop writer's block. If that happens, turn off your PC and blame it on a power failure.

Although Phil (CameraGod) had an active sex life, he considered himself a sexual bore. He never engaged in much foreplay and was sexually rigid. He had a limited repertoire of sexual fantasies. When he went online, he found himself luring women into private chats with the intention of having a sexual exchange. However, once he got to the private chat room, he didn't know where to go from there. Sex to him had always been a purely physical act. He had never expressed his sexual fantasies to anyone. With the help of some experienced online women, he began to communicate his sexual desires, forcing himself to move outside his rigid sexual boundaries. "It was a tremendous relief. I found myself sharing fantasies that I was too embarrassed to share before. My online encounters taught me about sexuality and the importance of trying new things to please myself and my partner."

Another interesting cybersexual phenomenon is the ever-growing popularity of dominance and submission (D/S) role-playing online. What is so captivating about this type of role-playing? It's the chance to practice a rather ancient form of sexual expression without the fear of being caught. Most of us conjure up whips and chains when we think about D/S encounters. However, fantasies and issues of power, control and trust fuel online D/S relationships. Some D/S encounters online do involve one individual using power and control to inflict emotional pain on a partner. As in real life, these types of sexual encounters can be quite psychologically damaging. However, there are also many individuals online who are active D/S players adhering to "safe play" by setting up guidelines and rules that must be strictly followed. These individuals institute "safe words" such as Safe, Sane and Consenting in their role-playing. They engage in D/S activities more as an opportunity to explore their sexual identity.

So, are there any dangers to this online phenomenon called cybersex? To begin with, cybersex sometimes catches newcomers off-guard, and they find themselves pressured to engage in cybersexual activities. It is easy to become caught up in the virtual reality of cyberspace. Some people falsely assume that their online behaviors do not carry much emotional weight in their real life. This is not true. Don't become involved in cybersexual encounters until you have assessed whether it is right for you. If you jump in too quickly, just as in real life, you will probably find yourself feeling regret. You also have to consider that your cybersexual partner may not be who you think he/she is. There are many individuals online who enjoy luring people into cybersexual relations by posing as someone they are not, only to reveal their true identity afterwards.

Kathy (Blond341) was 23 and looking for online romance. She was familiar with cybersex but wanted to save her **virtual virginity** for the right man. One evening she met Gary (Numbr-One) in the Hot Tub chat room. She felt an immediate attraction. He told her that he was 29 and working as an accountant. Their online relationship progressed quickly and she found herself, for the first time, engaging in cybersex. After several cybersexual encounters, Kathy began to push Gary for a phone number to further pursue the relationship. "I really felt close to Gary. I shared so many intimate thoughts and feelings with him. It seemed that we could be together in real life." After avoiding her requests several times, Gary finally confessed that he had not been honest with her about his age: He was actually 59. Kathy felt hurt and ashamed. She reported, "Never in real life would I have felt comfortable sharing my sexual fantasies with someone old enough to be my father!"

The fact that relationships may never develop beyond online contact disappoints some people who engage in cybersex. It is important to remember that many people engage in cybersex for pure fun, having no intention of taking the relationship further. But there are other individuals seeking a

virtual virginity. Reflects the fact that one has never engaged in cybersex over the Internet.

cyberphysical. A blending of the physical world with the imaginary world of cyberspace, such as that which takes place during cybersex.

cybermate. An individual's online partner in cyberspace. Some couples have online husbands (OH) and online wives (OW).

more intimate, lasting relationship. One of the dangers of cybersex is getting too emotionally involved with a partner who is viewing the encounter as purely **cyberphysical.** You may find yourself investing a great deal of emotional energy only to find that your partner has no intention of taking the relationship beyond the exchange of typed text. So, be careful if you are looking for more of a long-term commitment. As in real life, don't jump into sexual encounters too quickly. Be aware of your partner's intentions and ask questions.

Nancy (Bleueyes) found herself involved with a man online who shared similar interests and hobbies. As the relationship progressed, they moved to private chats that became more sexually intimate. Nancy expressed sexual fantasies that she had never shared before. She daydreamed about her cybermate and looked forward to any opportunity to be online with him. One day she clicked online to find that her **cybermate** had vanished, leaving no trail to follow. Nancy felt hurt and angry by the betrayal. "My deep feelings for this man surprised me. I gave so much of myself. It was devastating not being able to put closure on the relationship." Nancy had revealed her sexual soul and her lover had left her dangling in cyberspace. In the end, she learned a difficult lesson about sexual exploration online.

Not surprisingly, many married individuals are also having cybersex. The idea is appealing because many individuals find it easy to rationalize that cybersexual activities do not count as *real* affairs. Yet, digital relationships have destroyed many marriages. This issue will receive serious debate as the popularity of online services continues to expand.

His wife's involvement in a steamy cybersexual relationship shocked Paul. "One day I retrieved Kay's e-mails out of curiosity. I didn't expect to find correspondence from another man who said he looked forward to making love to her again in the hot tub! I wasn't sure how I should feel. Was she having an affair or not? While it was obvious that they had never met in real life, his e-mails were so intimate." Paul confronted his wife, but she minimized the significance of the relationship. She claimed that the relationship meant nothing and that her online encounters were merely fun and fantasy. Fearful of losing his wife, Paul gave in to her demands to continue her online activities. Six months later the marriage ended when Kay announced she was leaving him for a man she had met in cyberspace.

As in real life, marriages rarely tolerate any kind of third-party intrusion. There is a tendency for married individuals who engage in online affairs to minimize the emotional significance of these relationships. Consider whether it would bother you if you found out that your spouse was writing steamy love letters to someone else. Engaging in cybersex with someone is not very different. If your partner has a problem with your online sexual activity, it would be wise to respect his or her feelings. If you find yourself being secretive with your partner about your cybersexual activities, perhaps you should ask yourself why.

As online services continue to grow in popularity, more and more people will be engaging in sexual exchanges as they sit safely and comfortably behind their PCs. Cybersex is the modern-day marriage between technology and human sexuality. For many individuals it is a safe alternative to real-life sexual encounters, offering great freedom to expand one's repertoire of sexual behaviors. For others, engaging in cybersex may be damaging and pose significant emotional risks. In any event, cybersex requires some consideration on everyone's part.

SHARON'S STORY (Continued)

My husband took it amazingly well, and has been very supportive ever since I revealed my feelings for Pieter. Don't ask me how. We just talk, talk, talk about it whenever we need to, and everything has remained very open and honest. I have tried very hard to strike a balance we can live with, attempting to make both men feel loved and cherished and valued. I hope that I have succeeded for the most part.

Pieter didn't fare so well with his marriage. When his wife found out about us, she was devastated. Their marriage was nonexistent when I met Pieter, and he was trying to find a way out before he met me. He loves his son dearly, but is very unhappy with his wife and his marriage. This does not excuse us for what we have done, it merely explains how we allowed it to happen (us falling in love). We had some very difficult moments in our relationship. About six months after we fell in love, the heavy rush of overwhelming emotions began to abate, and the real work of making the relationship survive began. This happens in every love relationship, I think. It is the one thing that tests two people the most.

The sheer ridiculousness of it all, loving and needing and caring for someone we have never met face-to-face, threatens us constantly. The fact is very simple and plain: We love each other but even those words don't describe adequately how deeply we feel and how totally we are committed in our hearts to each other. We

SHARON'S STORY *(Continued)*

have "broken up," once for two miserable weeks, but our breakups are not because we stop getting along. They occur because we can't stand the separation from each other and we try to run from our pain, hoping that eventually our lives will heal from the hurt caused by being apart. We always come back together, though, smarter, more committed and stronger than we were before the breakup. We are even considering something so totally out of the norm, so impossible, that sometimes we can't even believe it ourselves. We are considering moving Pieter here to live in this house with my husband, daughter and myself. This is a terrifying prospect for all of us.

9

Caught in the Web

Subj: Possession of a soul!
From: Flamer999

   I don't sleep. I pay my AOL bill with mob-borrowed money. I have a port-a-potty next to me at all times. I lost my job, my wife, and forgot to feed my fish. I surf the Net so much that I can only focus my eyes on the monitor. But then, what else matters but the computer? She is my friend and confidante. I love how she chirps to life at the touch of a switch. Regardless of her cold gray shell, I know she really cares about me. Oh, did I tell you: I also have a pet. It's a mouse. I don't have to feed it, I just double click it!

Subj: Really addicted
From: JHYYSON

   You know when your addiction gets really bad is when you start buying wigs for your monitor. I was just looking at a blonde one the other day . . . help!!!!!!

Subj: Glued to the Web
From: Coolboy33

   Help! Get me off this crazy thing. This is like a drug. I don't pay for it myself; I am only 14 years *old. My mother pays on her credit card and allows me 10 hours a month. It is about $40 a month with service charge and all, but I usually go over my limit because I can't peel myself away from the keyboard. My parents are divorced so I am only at my mom's house (where my computer is) every other day. I come home from school, run straight to my computer and check my e-mail. On the days I'm at my dad's, I almost feel what you call withdrawal!!!!! I think about AOL and all the mail I might be missing all the time. Sometimes, and this will sound really lame, I even type my friend's notes on my dad's computer just to be with a keyboard. And it's not like I am some kind of computer dork. I have a good and fulfilling social life. It just goes to show you it can happen to anybody.*

That's how the story goes. Before you know it, you're caught in the Web. There are numerous stories of individuals who feel the same way. What starts off as innocent curiosity becomes a daily fixation. Your first visit online provides that initial rush. You can't believe the simplicity of the online services that make surfing a breeze and even more enticing. Before you know it, you feel like a master of cyberspace. You have a wealth of information and endless human contacts at your fingertips. Every time you sign on, your experience is different.

So, is it possible to become a Webaholic? Many kinds of behaviors can become obsessions. Being online is no exception. Here are some reasons why it's easy to become addicted to online services.

First, going online provides a source of immediate gratification. In other words, it feels good right away. Nowhere else can you instantly connect with an endless number of people quite like or different from yourself. Just a click of a button and you can immerse yourself in conversation with people all around the world. Each chat room is like a party with its own special theme. Click and choose which party you want to attend for the evening. There is no need to leave home. When it comes to a dress code, anything will do. You can sit in your underwear if you please!

If boring chat confronts you, move on to the next party. The parties are plentiful in cyberspace. The instant availability of social connection makes online services hard to resist, especially if you are the type of person who has difficulty meeting people in real life.

The anonymity of online services also proves addictive. People report feeling great freedom to say what they want to say without fear of rejection or criticism. In cyberspace you can speak your mind with little concern about how others will perceive you. Your unconscious becomes conscious as the interpersonal barriers of face-to-face interaction crumble. Think of it as a chance to free-associate with the keyboard, allowing your **cyber-id** to speak freely! Sitting at your PC you feel liberated, especially if you have a tendency to be emotionally rigid and tentative in face-to-face interactions. There is no holding back in cyberspace. Please, remember to mind your **cybermanners**!

cyber-id. Refers to one's more basic and primitive drives. In cyberspace, these drives are less governed and more likely to be freely expressed.

cybermanners. The use of proper respectful behavior while online. Also known as netiquette.

Once your relationships online become more permanent, nothing becomes more enticing than waiting to hear from fellow cybernauts via e-mail. You turn on your computer with great anticipation, hoping someone has sent correspondence. The intermittent reinforcement of e-mail (sometimes you have it, sometimes you don't), much like a slot machine, becomes instantly addictive! One feels compelled to go online often to see if e-mail is awaiting. There is no more anticipation of special holidays or events to hear from people in faraway places. E-mail is effortless! It's easy to sustain contact with the people you meet online no matter how far away they are. Once you become socially established in cyberspace, your e-mail will probably start to pile up. Essentially you can generate as much e-mail as you care to from your cyberfriends! The people willing and ready to extend their hands in cyberspace are endless.

Online services also become addictive in that they provide a temporary departure from the daily trials and tribulations of life. Cyberspace is a place to hide and forget responsibilities. Just like drugs and alcohol, there is the temporary escape factor. Turn on your PC and away you go! Your mind is momentarily free of worries, problems and ruminations. Many men and women view their online time as a time of relaxation, a time to chat or read about other people's experiences without the expectations that come with real-life relationships. However, you can only stay suspended in this virtual land for so long. Reality is always around the corner. Individuals who have a tendency to avoid the realities of life (paying bills, going to work), are especially prone to **Webaholism.**

So, how do you know if you have turned into a Webaholic? Here is a list of 15 signs of an Internet addiction that shed some humor on perhaps a not so humorous topic:

You know you're an addict when:

1. Instead of calling you to dinner, your spouse sends e-mail.
2. You walk into a room and, finding that it has more than 20 people, you inform the management that there is an error.
3. You **"ping"** people to see if they're awake, **"finger"** them to find out how they are, and **"AYT"** them to make sure they're listening to you.
4. You find yourself tilting your head when you smile.
5. You introduce your wife as "mylady@home.wife."
6. At social functions you introduce your husband as "my domain server."
7. You think that :) is your mirror image.
8. The only way your dog can get you to take him out for a walk is if he sets up his own home page.
9. When laughing, you find yourself saying "LOL" out loud.

Webaholism. Addiction to the Internet.

ping. A signal sent through cyberspace to determine lag time between you and someone else.

finger. An Internet program that allows you to check who is logged on to a specific host and to check whether or not a particular account exists.

AYT. Are you there?

10. If you are a male and see a female in the real world that you wish to meet, your first thought is to IM her.
11. If you are a female and see a male in the real world that you wish to meet, your first thought is that you wish he'd IM you.
12. When looking at signs, you wonder why they are always yelling at you.
13. When leaving to go to the bathroom, you find yourself saying "**BRB**."
14. Your spouse now complains of you moving your fingers in your sleep instead of talking.
15. When you have sex, sexually transmitted diseases no longer concern you.

BRB. Be right back.

On a more serious note, it is important to recognize if and when you have gone overboard online. Unfortunately, there are many individuals who have suffered serious consequences related to their online addiction. Some of these consequences are common to other types of addictions. For example, many people report tremendous financial problems because they can't kick the habit. Webaholics spend hundreds of dollars per month to feed their addiction. They report using online services much more often than what they originally intended. Real addicts stay online for up to 10 hours or more a day. Any attempts to cut down or regulate their online time is futile. These individuals also report taking extreme measures to obtain all the free online time they can. They fall into the trap of revolving their daily activities around the use of the computer. They ignore important social, occupational or recreational activities because of their online addiction. Feelings of isolation from friends and family are common. Many spouses of online addicts complain that they feel they have lost their mate to the world of cyberspace.

> *My IRC involvement has affected my life because of all the interesting people I have met online. I find myself thinking all day long about the people that I have met in cyberspace. When I get home from work the first thing I want to do is sign on and talk to the people I have come to know so well. I find myself daydreaming of the people that I have encountered and wonder what it would be like to meet them in person. I have never actually met anyone from my online encounters, but I have talked to one person on the phone. My husband is very jealous of my PC because I spend more time with it than with him.*
>
> *What I find so appealing about being online is that you can just be yourself. You don't have to hide behind fancy clothes, makeup and hairdos. You can just sit in front of your PC and it doesn't matter what you look like. I have to admit that I have lied once or twice (okay, maybe more than that) about what I look like. The only thing I have really lied about is how much I weigh. Here no one can judge me for being overweight. I can talk to almost anyone about anything.*

I know I am addicted to online services. Really I am. All I do is eat, sleep, work, and dream about the interesting people I have met online. All I want to do in my spare time is log on.

Much like a drug or alcohol addiction, Webaholics feel powerless and out of control. They can see that their behavior is negatively affecting their everyday existence, yet they continue to sign on. Webaholics often get feedback from significant others that they need to cool their jets, but still they can't. They are truly caught in the Web, tangled in the world of cyberspace that is boundless. The intensity of emotion in being an online addict becomes apparent in this posting.

Cateyes2 wrote: *Yes, okay (sob), I am an online junkie. I roam from site to site, begging for scraps of human interaction. I feel powerless over my machine. My mind is spinning and I can't seem to stop this addiction of mine. HELP ME (sob). Sometimes I steal someone's really fast modem and cruise the Web for days until I crash. So I ask (sob), can anyone relate? Am I the only one??? (sob)*

Despite their awareness of these problems, true Webaholics can't seem to pry themselves away from their computers. They express feeling compelled to sign on. Cybersneek wrote: "This is getting really serious for me! I cannot walk past my computer without going online. I haven't been out of the house for two days. I'm smoking more than ever. One last thing: That commercial that comes on TV for online services, 'WELCOME,' well, when I hear that, I automatically go into a trance-like state. I shuffle over to my computer, embrace it, and quickly sign on. I NEED HELP!!! WHAT CAN I DO?"

So, who out there may be susceptible to online addiction? Individuals who are looking to fulfill certain unmet needs may be likely candidates. For example, there are individuals who need excessive nurturing and guidance from others; individuals who look to online relationships for a sense of bonding, guidance and support. Let's refer to these individuals as **guidance seekers.** Guidance seekers look for feedback online in hopes of finding the direction they crave in life. Left to their own devices, they often have difficulty making decisions and choices in real life. They are afraid of assuming responsibility and rely upon others to tell them what to do. In cyberspace, it is easy to detect guidance seekers. Visit any chat room or bulletin board and you will see these individuals who are desperate in their search for direction. Fellow cybernauts who enjoy giving advice and feeling needed bombard them with suggestions and advice. Guidance seekers become quickly addicted to the amount of feedback they can receive in a short amount of time. There is great comfort in knowing that someone is always there to tell you what to do next. Unlike real life, if one fellow cybernaut tires of their neediness, they can always find someone else to listen.

> **guidance seekers.** Individuals who need excessive nurturing and guidance from others. They look to online relationships for a sense of bonding, guidance and support.

Gerry (Chaos113) found herself spending hours online. She found that her cyber-relationships filled a void in her life. "In cyberspace, I'm never alone. There is always someone there to listen and understand. It's hard to believe that there are so many people online willing to lend a helping hand." Gerry had always been especially close to her mother who was a strong and controlling woman. Her father was an alcoholic who died when she was 18. She felt a tremendous responsibility to take care of her mother following his death. At age 27 she still lived with her mother and struggled in making decisions about her future. Online services provided her the social connections for which she longed. However, she became quite dependent upon these relationships.

Gerry gravitated toward individuals with strong personalities, much like her mother, who would solve problems and provide suggestions. Although the relationships provided companionship and lessened her anxiety of being alone, she recognized that her online addiction also perpetuated her dependent behaviors. Gerry expressed, "I wish I could stand on my own two feet. Even online I find it hard to think for myself. I am always interested in what others have to say, but never give myself much credit for my thoughts."

social seekers. Isolated people who have a difficult time socially connecting in the real world.

There are also individuals who are in need of companionship. These are the **social seekers,** isolated people who have a difficult time socially connecting in the real world. These individuals try to meet all of their needs for intimacy online, making the addictive component very real. They scan the personals, do frequent postings and hang out in chat rooms for hours on end. The many social opportunities presented by the Internet captivate them. Their behavior online, interestingly, is often as socially awkward as it is in real life. Yet, in the world of cyberspace, social seekers are less likely to face criticism regarding their unpolished behavior. Instead, other users typically meet them with support and encouragement.

Larry (ShyOne) spent up to six hours a day in online chat rooms. He was an intensely shy individual in real life, avoiding social interactions at all cost. He worked the night shift as a supervisor in a factory and spent hours during the day in front of his computer. Larry's strong need for interpersonal connection conflicted with underlying fears of rejection and ridicule. Online services became a safe haven. He could hang out in the chat rooms and remain anonymous. The anxiety he often felt in being with people dissipated in cyberspace. Exposing his thoughts and beliefs seemed less threatening online. Others generally met him with encouragement and support. "I felt greater control in my online relationships. I could always sign off when I felt there was a threat of mockery or criticism. In cyberspace it seemed okay to be me. I found people more accepting."

Webaholics are also individuals who use their online experiences as a catharsis. Every time these individuals go online, they purge themselves of unwanted emotion. **Catharsis seekers**

catharsis seekers. Individuals who use their online experiences to purge themselves of unwanted emotion.

have difficulty finding a healthy outlet for their feelings in the real world, perhaps because their emotions are more intense than the average person. They are extreme in their opinions and look to prey on individuals who will absorb their extreme ideals and beliefs. Addiction comes easily because being online provides some cleansing of unwanted feelings. Catharsis seekers move from chat rooms to bulletin boards, leaving their emotional baggage in their wake.

James (Uzi1) is often described as hostile, resentful and extreme in his thinking. He grew up with a wealthy father who dictated his life and continued to control him with money. His mother was a shy, passive woman for whom James felt little respect. James lived alone and had no social contacts. His anxiety and rage—prompted by years of abuse and ridicule by his father—crippled him. His only connection with people was via the computer. Online, James asserted his extreme political views and ideas about morality. He took great freedom in being able to express what he wanted without serious consequence. Discharging unwanted emotion became his primary purpose for going online. He spent hours reading postings and responding with aggressive attacks. James also spent a great deal of time in chat rooms looking to provoke hostile exchanges. He changed his screen name frequently to avoid the people he angered.

Another category of online addicts is **control seekers.** Control seekers feel very little control in the real world. When real life becomes stressful

control seekers. Individuals who feel very little control in the real world. They experience greater control online.

and overwhelming, they run to their PC to escape. They feel greater control in the world of cyberspace where they can click their mouse and more easily determine an outcome. Relationships seem less complicated. There is less accountability, little to organize and less on which to follow up. Control seekers have difficulty expressing themselves in the real world. Emotions feel unsafe and frightening to them. They pay great attention to detail and frequently obsess about things. Online you will find them in chat rooms that are more intellectual. Perhaps they spend most of their time scrolling through bulletin boards and posting replies. Addiction also comes easily for the "control seeker" who is usually battling the complexity of emotional experiences in real life.

Penny (Pengirl) worked as a bookkeeper and lived with her husband and eight-year-old son. Her marriage had been in trouble for many years. Sharing herself emotionally with anyone was difficult. Penny worked long hours and obsessed over tasks. Perfectionism ruled her life. When she felt herself losing control of things or feeling emotionally overwhelmed, she ran to her computer to escape. She spent hours online involved in various alternative newsgroups which reflected her interest in cooking and books. She read hundreds of postings each week and wrote detailed responses about favorite recipes and novels she had read. She avoided chat rooms because they required more spontaneous interaction. Penny enjoyed the newsgroups that kept useful information and tips neatly organized. "At night I find that I can relax in front of my computer screen. Some of the newsgroups have become addictive for me. I enjoy the intellectual exchanges without the pressure to maintain ongoing relationships."

Whatever you are searching for online, be careful not to go overboard. Addiction to online services is truly problematic for some people. If you notice that your time online is starting to affect your work, home life, social life or finances, try to cut back. Perhaps you need to assess why you are spending excessive hours online. Are you lonely, bored in your marriage or perhaps shy? What needs are being met online that are not being fulfilled in real life? The following is a list of behavioral signs of online addiction. If three or more of these symptoms apply to your situation, you may need to consider seeking professional assistance.

1. You find yourself repeatedly spending more time online than you initially intended.
2. Attempts to cut back your time online have been futile.
3. When you are not online you find yourself mentally preoccupied with thoughts about being online and when you will have the next opportunity to do so.
4. Being online excessively has interfered with your employment (e.g., arriving to work late, difficulty focusing on work

because thoughts about being online pre-occupy your mind, spending time at work online when your boss has prohibited it).

5. You avoid usual social activities to be online.
6. Friends or family complain that you are spending too much time online.
7. Spending more and more time online does not seem to satisfy the desired effect of being online.
8. You spend more money than you can afford being online.
9. You are secretive about the amount of time you spend online.

Addiction to online services is becoming increasingly common. Check out the **Internet Addiction Support Group (IASG)** if you have concerns about your online behavior. You can subscribe to the IASG by e-mail: Address: listserv@netcom.com Subject: (leave blank). Message: Subscribe i-a-s-g. Another alternative is the **Webaholics Support** home page (http://www.ohiou.edu/~rbarrett/webaholics/), where you can find some comfort in commiserating with other Webaholics. There is also a **World Headquarters of Netaholics Anonymous** located at http://www.safari.net/~pam/netanon/.

SHARON'S STORY *(Continued)*

Pieter and I will meet in Scotland in one month to decide, finally, if this is all real. After a year's worth of love and pain and tears and devotion, we believe it is. We shall see. I have no idea what the future holds beyond that. I am not even trying to imagine where this will all lead. I have fantasies of how it might be if we can finally be together. Pieter does, too. However, we are both smart enough to know that fantasy and reality bear little resemblance to one another.

All I know is that I am a different person today than I was on the day I met Pieter. I think he is a different person, too.

10

Beta Testing

Relationships on the Internet take on as many forms as those in the real world. People become addicted, have affairs, fall in love, develop friendships and experience conflict. Each intimate connection has its own unique character and with each relationship formed online comes a story. Some stories are very short; perhaps a line or two. For others, the story turns into a novel that continues for months or perhaps years.

These connections are, for the most part, text-based exchanges. Chats and e-mails dominate the world of the Net. All of that will change as technology develops new and more sophisticated ways in which to communicate. Much of it is already here.

Audio compression makes it possible to speak over the Internet in real time. Mass use of video conferencing is not far off in the future. Now you'll be able to see to whom you're talking. The imagination isn't going to have to work as hard in the future. What's the next step? Possibly, it is a tactile medium. Perhaps it will include olfactory sensation and taste someday. It will be a virtual experience indeed.

Let's take a peek into the future and get an idea of what that might look like:

The Time: The not-so-distant future.

The Place: Wallaby's, an Australian virtual bar in cyberspace.

Enter our cybernauts.

Michael (MA) 34, single, engineer, lives in Miami, Florida

Sandy (SM) 32, single, attorney, lives in Sydney, Australia

Michael flips on his multimedia, fiber-optic computer. He's had a tough day and wants to wind down a bit, so he decides to spend some time at Wallaby's. He likes the way they've set up the room and the people who hang out there. He moves his mouse through the room looking left then right. Michael notices that they've done some redecorating since he was there last. Sandy's already arrived. She's chatting in the room using text that has each member's live or static picture to the left of their text. Fellow cybernauts from Spain, Italy, Sri Lanka, Japan, the U.S. and of course Australia greet Michael. Gina from Italy doesn't speak any English but that doesn't matter since her computer translates the text for her. Others see what she says in the language of their choice while she reads everything they say in Italian.

After giving him a few minutes to settle in, Sandy catches Michael's attention and asks him if he'd like to go "virtual private." She met Michael in Wallaby's a few weeks ago, liked him and wanted to get to know him better. He agrees but asks her to wait a second so that he can change. Fine with her, she'd like to freshen up, too.

A few moments later they meet "live." He finds that she's attractive and has a pleasant voice. She thinks he's better looking live than in his static image. Sandy comments on his sunburn, and he teases her about her Aussie accent. They spend a few hours flirting, kidding around and getting to know each other. Michael goes to sleep that night thinking about sex, and wishing that the R&D people at Sony would hurry and get those virtual gloves to the mass market so that he could "feel" Sandy's body. Sandy goes to sleep wishing Michael wasn't over 8,000 miles away, but happy she met him.

Far off in the future you think? Don't blink! It's right around the corner.

In cyberspace, now and increasingly in the future, time and distance become less and less of an obstacle that separates people. New software will eliminate language barriers. Individuals around the globe will share the richness of cultural diversity in new and interesting ways. Exploring the world will be a question of simply deciding where you want to go.

People already have relationships that never would have developed without the Internet. The geographically and socially isolated are finding a new way to connect intimately. Encounters by the thousands are taking place every day between people who would never have possibly met under normal circumstances. Chance meetings across town or across oceans abound.

Where is the technology of the Internet leading us? The world is already a very impersonal place.

Don't Internet relationships further reduce the meaning of human interactions to the level of a button and graphic interfaces? Will increasing reliance on technology dominate the relationships of the future? Won't people decide to stay in rather than venture out of the home to meet others? Will face-to-face communication disappear?

This is not likely. Relationships on the Internet will continue to be just another way to connect, not a replacement for face-to-face relationships. Nature did not biologically or psychologically design us to live in sterile environments where all we do is relate through a modem. Such a view of human nature would be sadly shortsighted and simplistic. Technology is a powerful force but one that can't replace the complexity of human interaction. The Internet can get us together, but that's all. What happens after that is up to us.

We can view the Internet as a medium of communication that lies somewhere between the passivity of TV and the full experience of real life. Relationships in cyberspace involve participation. Perhaps most importantly, venturing into cyberspace is a choice. One can choose to relate to others through this medium or not. Whether you like it is really a matter of personal choice. It would be a mistake to condemn a communication technology that has brought so much to so many. In any case, whether we like it or not, the revolution is here.

Beta testing refers to the final stage of product development before general release. It is a level of refinement where the designers identify and

---

beta testing. The final stage of product development before general release. The goal is to identify and correct all bugs and problems so all parts work smoothly together to achieve a desired goal.

hopefully correct the bugs and problems. The goal of beta testing is a relationship among parts that work smoothly together to achieve a desired goal.

Relationships on the Internet, whether friendships, romantic or sexual, will always be in the beta testing stage as the possibilities are endless. Sometimes they run smoothly and sometimes they don't. Each experience will be unique and in a state of continual evolution, just like anything else that's alive.

Remember this: As the Internet continues to expand technologically and the number of users increases, the world will continue to shrink. This is the secret of why the Internet is so attractive to millions of users. Humans have a need and a desire to intimately connect to each other, not just to a source of information.

Do intimate connections on the Internet enhance your life? You'll have to do your own beta testing to answer that!

APPENDIX: SELF-QUIZ

Are you in a reflective mood? Here's a self-quiz designed to help give you an idea of your level of involvement in online relationships. Some individuals are casually involved while others are heavily engaged in their online world. Which grouping describes you? Simply read each question and circle the appropriate column for *True* or *False*. Add up the total number of *True* responses to find your score.

In a chat room, I'd be more likely to introduce myself than wait for someone to approach me.	T	F
I do not have at least one friend in which I can confide everything.	T	F
I generally trust others online.	T	F
I tend to move very slowly online with self-disclosure.	T	F
I like the anonymity of the Internet.	T	F
Online friendships are important to me.	T	F
I frequently check to see if my cyberfriends are online.	T	F

It would annoy me if I saw my nickname used by someone else on the Internet.	T	F
If I saw my nickname in a chat room that offended me, it would bother me.	T	F
I consider myself to be a reserved person in real life.	T	F
I e-mail at least one to five people over the Internet regularly.	T	F
I e-mail more than five people over the Internet regularly.	T	F
I have a GIF of my own that I send out over the Internet on occasion.	T	F
It's difficult to meet people and make friends where I live.	T	F
I have experienced or am looking for romance online.	T	F
I have experienced or am looking for friendship online.	T	F
I have experienced or am looking for cybersex online.	T	F
I spend at least three hours per week in either public or private chats.	T	F
I spend between three and six hours per week in public or private chats.	T	F
I spend more than six hours per week in public or private chats.	T	F

Score

0–5: You're likely to find relationships in cyberspace superficial and fleeting. You tend to view them casually, perhaps as a form of entertainment. You're probably an occasional cruiser of chat rooms and perhaps have an occasional online relationship.

6–10: You're likely to be an individual who is social offline and has at least a few meaningful relationships with others. You tend to enjoy relating to others in cyberspace and have developed or will develop a few ongoing relationships on the Internet that you consider to be true friendships. At the same time, you may spend hours online chatting with others during a single session and may not return to a chat room for weeks.

11–15: You are probably an individual who views his online relationships as personally meaningful and serious. You are likely to devote many hours to online public and private chats, and exchanges of e-mail. Telephone calls, trading of GIFS and occasional IRL meetings are common forms of additional contact.

16–20: It is likely that you are heavily involved in the social fabric of the Internet. You probably have a large number of online relationships or have online relationships that are emotionally intimate. If you are in this group, you may "know" over 50 fellow cybernauts, or you may have relationships that are intense and very meaningful. Many cyber-romances are included here as they are characterized by a great deal of time online coupled with the intensity of the emotional experience.

From the standpoint of emotional vulnerability, disappointments affect people who score in the lower ranges less. Higher scoring individuals are more vulnerable as they invest more emotion in their online relationships. Increasing involvement on the Net tends to raise expectations. When our relationships meet or exceed these expectations, we're pleased. When they don't meet our expectations, we're disappointed and frustrated. Mid-level scores typify many online users who enjoy much of what online relationships may have to offer while not being too negatively affected by the disappointments that can take place there.

FAQs FROM CYBERSPACE

All kinds of relationships exist in cyberspace. Many represent brief encounters lasting only a few moments that have little or no meaning. Others develop into relationships that span months and even years and are rich in meaning. Online users establish friendships, kindle romances, spark affairs and find support.

Public and private chat rooms, news groups, GIFs and e-mails provide the means to an end involving an endless network of human interaction.

Millions of exchanges take place every day and are increasing at a phenomenal rate. All of this activity can be hard to follow. The new experience of relating to others online raises many questions. What are the rules of behavior on the Internet? Is a cyberaffair a real affair? Are relationships over the Net real? Can I really trust anyone over the Net?

Before we answer these and other specific questions, it's important to understand a key point: *the bigger picture.*

The interactive social matrix of the Internet serves a deeper purpose than simply satisfying *individual needs*. It also serves the *collective needs* of our species. Our survival requires a cooperative effort to insure we meet our drives for food, defense, nurturing of our young and reproduction. Psychologically, human beings have a need to socialize. This desire to socialize helps us work together to meet our collective needs.

Friendships, romance, cybersex and support online are just another way to connect us. These connections do of course represent a new way in which to relate. The Internet is a new *form* of communication but the *purpose* is timeless. The rules of behavior on the Internet are evolving and will change as a function of new technological developments. What will *not* change is the *drive* to connect. When we understand this, then we realize that the infinite connections that can take place in cyberspace are all variations on the same theme. The rules of behavior are simply rough guides to a road with endless turns. The scenery constantly changes but the road moves us forward.

FAQs. Frequently asked questions.

With this in mind, let's answer some **FAQs** about relationships on the Net.

Q: Are online relationships real?

A: Relationships formed over the Net are indeed *real* to the vast majority of users. They become *more* real as they progress from text to phone to IRL meetings. The nature of the medium does, however, permit easy exaggeration and misrepresentation of fact. Alter egos exist in cyberspace and are often very difficult to detect. As many online relationships move on to more direct contact, reality replaces the projected fantasy of the other individual. Sometimes reality enhances the fantasy, while other times it frustrates the fantasy. This can be especially true in cases involving online romance.

Q: How do I meet people online?

A: IRC chat rooms on the Internet and commercial carriers such as AOL are popular places to meet. The various BBSs are also popular meeting grounds. As in the real world, many online relationships form from an initial random encounter in cyberspace. The rule of thumb is to allow oneself time to get to know the theme of the chat room or BBS you're visiting. Also, a basic grounding in Netiquette and the use of **emoticons** will help.

Q: What are the rules of behavior on the Internet?

A: The usual rules of social interaction don't really apply over the Net. The medium is primarily text-based at this time, so the typical subtleties that influence the flow of interaction between people are missing. You can't *see* how someone just reacted to what you've said in cyberspace. You have to wait for their text or e-mail. The immediacy

emoticon. Computer symbols used to denote the spirit of a line of typed text.

of face-to-face or even phone contact lends itself to a wider range of responsive behavior. Behavior over the Net is, in this sense, much more restrictive since the Net limits the range of expression to text. This will, of course, change radically as audio and video are introduced on a large scale. In cyberspace, there are really no rules except those which govern general interaction, including respect for others and so forth. A rough guide for behavior on the Net, referred to as Netiquette, is simply the application of principles of proper respectful behavior as translated to the medium of the Net. In many ways, the Internet represents a *wild west* of human interactivity. When rules are hard to enforce through social disapproval and personal responsibility, the possibility of crossing usual social bounds increases. Many individuals feel safe and anonymous behind a PC and a screen name.

Q: Can alter egos develop unintentionally?

A: Yes. The Internet as it stands today is an easy medium in which to present an alter ego. The text-based interactions that currently dominate online relationships allow for easy alter ego development. There are many fiction writers on the Net. A simple keystroke such as stating one is single when really married can start the ball rolling toward the presentation of an entire alter ego. The best way to avoid falling into the trap of lying on the Net is very simple: Always tell the truth.

Q: How can I tell if I'm talking to an alter ego?

A: Very often you can't. However, there are some signs to look for. Be aware of consistency in the individual's stories about him or herself. Also, alter egos tend to embellish stories quite a bit. How likely is it that the guy you're chatting with online really is a multimillionaire son of a sultan who happens to be in the United States on a Rhodes scholarship working aggressively on a cure for cancer? If the relationship progresses further, alter egos are very reluctant to give out their home telephone numbers. This is often the case with married individuals who claim they are single.

Q: Am I always talking to a real person?

A: Not in all cases. Some individuals have set some computers to respond to chats in a predetermined fashion depending upon what the *real* person is typing online. A number of these programs are quite sophisticated. It can take some time to determine that you are chatting with a computer. One tip to help you tell the difference is to repeat the same question twice and check the response.

Q: Aren't all cybernauts socially awkward in real life?

A: Far from it. The Internet continues to grow at a remarkable pace because proprietary carriers such as AOL attract more and more mainstream users. Men and women from all walks of life participate in this virtual community. A popular myth is that Internet users are socially awkward individuals who have a found safe place to interact without having to risk a *real* relationship. While it's true that shy people can find it more comfortable to socialize in Cybercheers, the majority of users are socially adept and simply enjoy the Internet as another way to connect.

Q: Can I really find romance online?

A: Yes. Many thousands of couples have met online and their relationships have progressed to the point of marriage. As in the real world, however, individuals experience many disappointments as well. As always, it's best to proceed cautiously in cyberspace as the medium poses many opportunities and challenges.

Q: Can I really trust anyone over the Net?

A: Yes. Men and women form many meaningful and long-term relationships over the Internet. Remember that experience and time enhance trust. As relationships become more intimate, they usually progress to phone contact and IRL meetings. It's best to be somewhat guarded in the beginning and allow yourself to open up over time, while your cyberspace partner does the same. The best relationships are those characterized by a sense of equity in which both individuals feel they are receiving something reasonably proportional to what they give. Still, there are no guarantees that someone will not violate your trust. If your threshold for disappointment is very low, it's best that you keep your contacts in cyberspace light and superficial.

Q: What is cybersex?

A: Cybersex is the exchange of erotic text designed to stimulate another partner in cyberspace. The use of language is often creative, and users may supplement it with GIFs. Since cybersex involves such a powerful fantasy component, many users find it to be a highly erotic experience. Often individuals explore fantasies online that they would never express in real life.

Q: Are cyberaffairs real affairs?

A: The answer to this question depends on whom you ask. Most online users maintain that cyberaffairs are nothing more than a harmless erotic diversion. Offline partners are more likely to view them as a definite violation of the primary relationship. If an individual limits the cyberaffair to online contact only, it's difficult to argue that it is equivalent to an IRL fling. At the same time, many significant others view it as a violation of the marital relationship. What seems to be a more important issue is how the couple responds to such an experience. Some couples view it as an erotic enhancement to their relationship. Some partners even enjoy watching the interchange take place online. In other cases, it can cause great stress in a relationship to the point of a breakup.

Q: How do I deal with the fact that my partner is having a cyberaffair?

A: The most important factor in dealing with such an issue in the relationship is to communicate about it. For some couples, the cyberaffair represents nothing more than a harmless form of erotic entertainment that can enhance their sex lives. For others, the cyberaffair represents a violation of trust and can be a serious threat to the relationship. It's important to understand that in these cases, the cyberaffair crosses the boundary that surrounds and protects the relationship. The partner engaged in the online affair should respect the wishes of his partner and end the online relationship. The couple should then determine what the cyberaffair provided. Was there something missing in the relationship that created the conditions to look elsewhere? Men typically will engage in a cyberaffair for much the same reasons they do in the real world, that is, in search of sexual excitement. Women, on the other hand, are more likely to be in search of intimacy and friendship. In any case, online lovers tend to be very attentive and nearly everyone wants attention.

Q: What is a sudden loss in cyberspace?

A: A sudden loss in cyberspace occurs when a relationship abruptly ends without warning. An example might be an intimate cyberaffair that spans many months and hundreds of chats that comes to a halt when a spouse finds out about the affair. A search in cyberspace is fruitless. The online lover never hears from her beloved again. This can be, of course, emotionally upsetting to one or both parties especially if the relationship was an intimate and meaningful one. It's best to be cautiously optimistic about relationships in cyberspace. Many users limit the responsibility they feel for the welfare of fellow cybernauts.

Q: Should I meet my online lover IRL?

A: Meeting an online lover IRL is a question of individual preference. Many individuals travel thousands of miles to finally meet. By the time two people plan such a meeting, there have been several phone calls and usually the exchange of GIFS or pictures via snail mail. Some individuals end up being disappointed while for others the meeting results in marriage. It is important to remember that while relationships over the Net can be exciting and interesting, the medium limits the information available to you about another person. The individual planning on an IRL meeting should expect that the meeting will happily surprise or disappoint. Online personas do not necessarily translate IRL.

Q: Doesn't time online take away from family life?

A: It can in many cases. Many individuals who do not spend time online complain that their partners spend many hours on the computer chatting away. Their concern is that family life will suffer. Spending too much time online (or excessive involvement in any activity, for that matter) is potentially destructive to a relationship. Time spent online can simply represent an enjoyable pastime for the user, or it may be a way to avoid problems in a relationship at home. As with almost everything in life, balance is important and cybernauts should be sensitive to the needs of their partners and families. Interestingly, as PCs evolve into multimedia centers, they will move from a corner of the den to the family room, where the possibility of family involvement increases. In the future, it will not be unusual for a family in Miami to converse in real time with a family in Australia they met online. We do not know what the sociopsychological implications of these types of changes in the way we interact will be. Spending time as a family with others online would serve as an active medium for family entertainment. Parents would probably view this more positively than television.

Q: How do I know if I'm addicted to Internet relationships?

A: Addicted may be a misnomer. Saying one is addicted to online relationships may be like saying one is socializing with others too much. As a rule, we can characterize any addiction as increased tolerance and withdrawal. Increased tolerance on the

Net means an individual spends more and more time online and experiences a sense of withdrawal when offline. Also, compulsive usage takes place when the user wants to stop but feels he or she cannot. Another definition of online addiction involves the idea that the online use interferes with occupational or social functioning. An example might be an individual whose spouse complains that he spends too much time online, or someone whose career is suffering from neglect due to too much time online.

Q: How do I stop if I do think I'm addicted?

A: Various online support groups exist to help individuals deal with their compulsive behavior. Proprietary providers such as AOL even have chat rooms devoted to the problem. A good way to cut down is to establish a specific schedule of online time such as an hour an evening and perhaps a quick check for e-mail in the morning. A moderate approach is more reasonable and more realistic than a radical one. Psychologically, staying away from the Net for a time is more likely to produce a rebound effect. The result is that usage is more likely to go up rather than down when you finally power up the PC.

Q: Isn't all the hype about Internet relationships just a fad?

A: The hype will pass but the revolution of the medium is here to stay. The Internet and the relationships formed there will continue to grow in popularity and sophistication. This is primarily due to one fact: The drive causing the explosive growth of these connections in cyberspace is the human need to establish relationships with others. It's that simple and at the same time that complicated. As with radio, telephone and television, any communication medium with the kind of power that the Internet has in connecting us is here to stay.

HOW IT WORKS

For many, the Internet is a mysterious, complex computer system that exists in cyberspace and is difficult to understand. The idea of accessing information and communicating across the country or around the world with other individuals over the Net is mind-boggling. As amazing as it is, engineers designed the Web on some basic principles. Here's how it works.

A *modem* connects individual computers to a *server* that provides access to the greater information superhighway. Think of modems as vehicles that have the capacity to travel at different speeds and servers as the on-ramps to the highway. Once you're on, you can go anywhere you want to in cyberspace.

One can choose a destination by either going directly there or consulting a directory that will list sites relevant to your interest such as active chat rooms. Some larger proprietary servers have chat rooms that you can only access through their system.

If you're looking for someone in particular, you can search cyberspace to see if they're out there somewhere. Then you can join them in a chat room or send them an instant private message.

You send these messages—as well as e-mail and GIFs—from site to site through a series of land- and satellite-based links.

For example, if you're in the U.S. chatting with someone in India, your link may involve relays through several servers. The lag time between the sending and receiving of a message is often quite short. It may take longer depending on a number of factors, including how much traffic exists in that section of the highway at that particular time. Yes, there are "rush hours" on the Net.

GLOSSARY

alter ego. A misrepresentation of actual factual personal data or personality characteristics.

Alt.newsgroups. Discussions on the Internet with an alternative or many times unclear theme.

AOL. America Online. One of the largest online services.

/action. Refers to a physical act, such as /action JC_ hands Janie a rose -(-(-(-(@.

BBS. Bulletin board service. A central computer that you can connect to via your modem that allows the user to post messages, chat, send e-mail and download files, programs and other information.

beta testing. The final stage of product development before general release. The goal is to identify and correct all bugs and problems so all parts work smoothly together to achieve a desired goal.

catharsis seekers. Individuals who use their online experiences to purge themselves of unwanted emotion.

chat room. A virtual room in cyberspace where individuals "gather" to discuss certain themes. Chat rooms can include as many as 20 or more people.

control seekers. Individuals who feel very little control in the real world. They experience greater control online.

cyberaffair. A virtual affair.

Cybercheers. A term we coined to capture the true spirit of cyberspace, to describe the spirit of the space behind your computer.

cyberdrink. An imaginative drink shared in cyberspace.

cyberfling. An online cybersexual interaction, usually of a casual nature.

cyberfriends. Those online individuals to whom a user has formed emotional attachments.

cyberhandle. An individual's unique online name or nick that often communicates something about that person.

Cyberia. A synonym for cyberspace.

cyber-id. Refers to one's more basic and primitive drives. In cyberspace, these drives are less governed and more likely to be freely expressed.

cybermanners. The use of proper respectful behavior while on-line. Also known as Netiquette.

cybermate. An individual's online partner in cyberspace. Some couples have online husbands (OH) and online wives (OW).

cybernauts. A term used to describe the people who are interacting on the Internet.

cyberphysical. A blending of the physical world with the imaginary world of cyberspace, such as that which takes place during cybersex.

cybersex. Online equivalent of engaging in sex in the real world. Individuals type out their sexual fantasies for the purpose of mutual stimulation.

cybershorthand. Acronyms and emoticons used online in place of complete phrases or sentences, i.e., BRB—be right back. LOL—laughing out loud.

cybersocial arena. The plane in cyberspace in which various relationships between people take place.

cybersocialites. Social leaders in cyberspace. They often act as hosts in chat rooms.

cyberspace. A popular term used to describe the virtual meeting place of people who are using telecommunication technology.

dependent. An individual who becomes overly attached to others in cyberspace.

e-mail. Electronically transmitted messages traveling from one computer to another.

emoticon. Computer symbols used to denote the spirit of a line of typed text.

FAQs. Frequently asked questions. Files posted for many Usegroups and services that contain questions and answers for the purpose of educating newcomers.

finger. An Internet program that allows you to check who is logged on to a specific host and to check whether or not a particular account exists.

flame. A nasty, insulting message sent via e-mail or postings usually telling the recipient that there has been a violation of Netiquette.

flame war. When two or more individuals begin exchanging flames, or insults, online.

GIF. Graphic interchange format used for image files. Most images found on the World Wide Web are in GIF format. Exchanging GIFs online commonly refers to the electronic exchange of personal photos.

guidance seekers. Individuals who need excessive nurturing and guidance from others. They look to online relationships for a sense of bonding, guidance and support.

hot chat. Online sex talk.

IM. Instant message. A command used to send a private message to someone else online.

IRC. Internet Relay Chat. A communications program that allows for real-time conversation between Internet users all over the world.

IRL. In real life.

list-serv. An online mailing list.

lurker. A visitor to a newsgroup or online service who observes communication between others but doesn't participate.

modem. A device connected to a computer or terminal that allows for transfer of data via a connection to a telephone line.

mouse. A small device connected to the computer which allows the user to navigate the cursor on the computer screen.

MUD. Multi-User Dungeon. Games played in real time on the Internet that involve multiple users who engage in adventure role-playing.

narcissist. An individual who cruises the net looking for attention from others.

Netiquette. Rules of etiquette that govern personal behavior online.

Netpals. Friends who connect online and continue their relationships through e-mail and other modes of Net communication. These are the online equivalent to snail-mail pen pals.

Netsex. Describes any activity over the internet with the purpose of erotic stimulation such as cybersex.

Netsurfer. An individual who most often cruises cyberspace with no particular destination in mind.

newbie. A newcomer to cyberspace.

newsgroups. Usenet conferences that are organized by topic. Users are free to post messages related to the topics.

one-night cyberstand. A brief cybersexual encounter that does not result in the development of any kind of meaningful relationship online or offline.

online. Interaction with a host computer via local or long-distance telecommunications.

PC. Refers to the personal computer, which is the basic hardware permitting the average individual to gain access to cyberspace.

ping. A signal sent through cyberspace to determine lag time between you and someone else.

posting. A message on a bulletin board.

profile. Select internet providers allow individuals to post personal information such as age, gender, interests, etc., for others to view.

SES. Stands for social economic strata, which is determined by factors such as income and profession. In cyberspace, all cybernauts are created equal . . . at least initially.

snail-mail. A term used in cyberspace to describe our conventional postal service delivery.

social seekers. Isolated people who have a difficult time socially connecting in the real world.

sociopath. A manipulative individual with little regard for others. The sociopath's sole purpose in being online is to use others to satisfy his needs only.

surfing. A leisure approach to exploring online areas of interest.

Undernet. A computer network that permits access to active chat rooms. Undernet connections may contain over 3,000 active rooms reflecting a wide variety of themes.

usenet groups. A list of discussion groups on the Internet.

virtual virginity. Reflects the fact that one has never engaged in cybersex over the Internet.

Webaholic. A person who is addicted to Internet usage. A webaholic may experience a need to spend increasingly long periods online that may interfere with social or occupational functioning.

Webmaster. An individual responsible for developing and maintaining a home page on the Internet.

World Wide Web. A synonym for the Internet.

MORE STORIES FROM THE NET!

Share your online relationship story for future works written by Dr. Adamse and Dr. Motta! Stories of romance, affairs, friendship and support are welcomed, as are your comments concerning this book. Send your story to:

Snail-mail:

>Michael Adamse, Ph.D.
>Sheree Motta, Psy.D.
>1515 N. Federal Hwy., Suite 404
>Boca Raton, Florida 33432
>FAX: 561-394-6273

or e-mail:

>Cyshrink@gate.net

To protect confidentiality, all identifying information will be deleted from stories. We also welcome you to our Cybershrink home page (http://www.gate.net/~cyshrink or http://www.cybershrink.com), where you can ask us questions about your online relationships. We look forward to hearing from you!

Wishing you much success online!

EMOTICONS

Emoticons are a form of cybershorthand that is used over the Internet to communicate an idea or emotion. Here are some of the more popular ones used to convey the spirit in which a line of text was typed. Hint: If you don't understand it, turn the page sideways.

:) smile

:(frown

{{{{}}}} hugs

#:) bad hair day

:* kiss

—-{—-{—-{—-@ long-stemmed rose

:-| disgusted

:-\/ shouting

: -(O) yelling

: -@ cursing

: b sticking tongue out

: '-(crying

% -) confusion

: - 0 uh-oh!

>: -> making a devilish remark

: -C feeling really bummed

: - / feeling skeptical

: I hmmm . . .

| -) hee hee

| -D ho ho

: -> hey hey

: -o oops

ACRONYMS

These acronyms are commonly used as savers of bytes of time in conversation online. To make the best impression while chatting you may want to memorize a few.

ASAP. As soon as possible.

AYT. Are you there?

BL. Belly laughing!

BRB. Be right back.

BTW. By the way.

DIKU. Do I know you?

F2F. Face to face.

FAQ. Frequently asked question.

FWIW. For what it's worth.

IM. Instant message.

IMCO. In my considered opinion.

IMHO. In my humble opinion.

IRL. In real life.

ISO. In search of (used frequently in member rooms).

LOL. Laughing out loud.

MOTOS. Member of the opposite sex.

MOTSS. Member of the same sex.

OH. Online husband.

OHinL. Online husband-in-law.

OIC. Oh, I see!

OTOH. On the other hand.

OW. Online wife.

OWinL. Online wife-in-law.

PITA. Pain in the "acronym."

PTMM. Please tell me more.

ROFL. Rolling on the floor laughing.

RTFM. Read the, uh, friggin' manual.

S/AC. Sex, age check.

WYSIWYG. What you see is what you get.

BIBLIOGRAPHY

American Psychiatric Association Staff. *Diagnostic & Statistical Manual of Mental Disorders: DSM-IV.* 4th ed. Washington, DC: American Psychiatric Association, 1994.

Barlow, John Perry. "Is There a There in Cyberspace?" *Utne Reader,* March-April, 1995: 53–56.

Barol, Bill. "What Is Cyberspace?" *VirtualCity,* Fall 1995: 26–34.

Hamilton, Kendall, and Claudia Kalb. "They Log On, But They Can't Log Off." *Newsweek,* December 18, 1995: 60–61.

Kornbluth, Jesse. "(You Make Me Feel Like) A Virtual Woman." *VirtualCity,* Winter 1996: 56–58.

Kupfer, Andrew. "Alone Together: Will Being Wired Set Us Free?" *Fortune,* March 20, 1995: 94–104.

Landis, David. "Love Online: Cyberspace as a Frontier for Romance." *USA Today,* February 11, 1994: 1.

Levy, Steven. "This Changes . . . Everything." *Newsweek,* December 25, 1995: 22-30.

Mandell, Tom. "Confessions of a Cyberholic." *Time* 145, no. 12 (Spring 1995): 57.

McClellan, Jim. "Confessions of an Online Junkie." *Newsday,* June 27, 1995: B23.

Millrod, Jack. "Life in Cyberspace: RSVP to a One-of-a-Kind Party." *Newsday,* May 16, 1995: B27.

Smolowe, Jill. "Intimate Strangers." *Time* 145, no. 12, (Spring 1995): 20–24.

Steinberg, Don. "Inside the Noisy World of Online Chat." *VirtualCity,* Winter 1996: 34–42.

Szalavitz, Maia. "Cyber-Nookie: When Is Online Sex Adultery?" *VirtualCity,* Fall, 1995: 19.

Toufexis, Anastasia. "Romancing the Computer." *Time,* February 19, 1996: 53.

Tough, Paul. "What Are We Doing Online?" *Harper's,* August, 1995: 35–46.

Van Der Leun, Gerard. "Twilight Zone of the Id." *Time* 145, no. 12, (Spring 1995): 36-37.

ABOUT THE AUTHORS

Michael Adamse, Ph.D.

Educated at the University of Miami and a pre-doctoral fellow at Yale University, Michael Adamse has published research on chronic drug abuse and served as Director of Psychology at a major psychiatric hospital. He holds an appointment as Adjunct Assistant Professor of Psychology at the University of Miami.

In 1986, Dr. Adamse started his private, specializing in relationship issues, including marriage counseling, divorce and the effects of relationship problems on children.

Sheree Motta, Psy.D.

Dr. Motta completed her graduate education at Nova Southeastern University in Florida, after undergraduate work at Georgetown College in Kentucky. She interned at Fairfield Hills Hospital in Connecticut and served as the Program Director of the Neurobehavioral Treatment Center at a major psychiatric hospital.

In private practice with Michael Adamse since 1990, Sheree Motta also specializes in relationship issues such as divorce, intimacy, communication, co-dependency and abuse.

Drs. Adamse and Motta founded the Institute for the Study of Internet Relationships. The Institute is dedicated to the understanding and exploration of online human interaction.

They can be reached at 1515 North Federal Hwy., Suite 404, Boca Raton, FL 33432, or call (561) 395-5654.

Now Is the Time to Bring That Loving Feeling Back into Your Relationship!

Coupling Audiocassette
Bring Back That Loving Feeling
Michael Adamse, Ph.D., and Sheree Motta, Psy.D.

The authors of *Online Friendship, Chat-Room Romance and Cybersex* provide you with the key to a relationship that is stronger, more passionate and more intimate. This 60-minute audiocassette is the equivalent of a crash course in communication from Drs. Adamse and Motta. These two expert clinical psychologists use a collection of examples, case studies and famous quotations to illustrate essential information you need to know to keep your intimate relationship healthy.

In *Coupling*, Adamse and Motta give the female and male perspective on love, communication, sex and trust, and offer practical and interesting suggestions to bring back that loving feeling in your relationship. They've based this sound psychological advice on 25 collective years of counseling individuals and couples with relationship problems.

By helping you to assess and strengthen your relationship, this dynamic yet practical tape is guaranteed to produce positive results in your relationship. You will discover the basic ingredients of a successful relationship and the spices that make it satisfying, all in the convenience of your home or car.

Code 40601AB **$11.95**

Available at your favorite bookstore or call 1-800-441-5569 for Visa or MasterCard orders. Prices do not include shipping and handling. Your response code is **BKS**.

Share the Magic of Chicken Soup

Chicken Soup for the Soul™
101 Stories to Open the Heart
and Rekindle the Spirit

The #1 *New York Times* bestseller and ABBY award-winning inspirational book that has touched the lives of millions. Whether you buy it for yourself or as a gift to others, you're sure to enrich the lives of everyone around you with this affordable treasure.

Code 262X trade paperback $12.95
Code 2913 hardcover $24.00
Code 3812 large print $16.95

A 2nd Helping of Chicken Soup for the Soul™
101 More Stories to Open the Heart and Rekindle the Spirit

This rare sequel accomplishes the impossible—it is as tasty as the original, and still fat-free. If you enjoyed the first *Chicken Soup for the Soul,* be warned: it was merely the first course in an uplifting grand buffet. These stories will leave you satisfied and full of self-esteem, love and compassion.

Code 3316 trade paperback $12.95
Code 3324 hardcover $24.00
Code 3820 large print $16.95

A 3rd Serving of Chicken Soup for the Soul™
101 More Stories to Open the Heart
and Rekindle the Spirit

The latest addition to the *Chicken Soup for the Soul* series is guaranteed to put a smile in your heart. Learn through others the important lessons of love, parenting, forgiveness, hope and perseverance. This tasty literary stew will stay with you long after you've put the book down.

Code 3790 trade paperback $12.95
Code 3804 hardcover $24.00
Code 4002 large print $16.95

Available at your favorite bookstore or call 1-800-441-5569 for Visa or MasterCard orders. Prices do not include shipping and handling. Your response code is **BKS**.

Hear the Heartwarming Goodness of Chicken Soup for the Soul™ on Audio

Health Communications, Inc. proudly presents its audio collection of the *Chicken Soup for the Soul* series. Each book is available on tape or CD for your convenience. Brighten your life by listening to these words of inspiration.

The Best of the Original Chicken Soup for the Soul™ Audio
Code 3723 one 90-minute cassette $9.95
Code 4339 one 70-minute CD $11.95

The Best of A 2nd Helping of Chicken Soup for the Soul™ Audio
Code 3766 two 90-minute cassettes $14.95
Code 4347 one 70-minute CD $11.95

The Best of A 3rd Serving of Chicken Soup for the Soul™ Audio
Code 4045 one 90-minute cassette $9.95
Code 4355 one 70-minute CD $11.95

Chicken Soup for the Women's Soul Audio
Code 4401 one 90-minute cassette $9.95
Code 441X one 70-minute CD $11.95

Chicken Soup for the Soul™ Audio Gift Set
Code 3103 6 cassettes, 7 hours $29.95

Chicken Soup for the Soul™ at Work Audio
Code 4428 one 90-minute cassette $9.95
Code 4436 one 70-minute CD $11.95

Available at your favorite bookstore or call 1-800-441-5569 for Visa or MasterCard orders. Prices do not include shipping and handling. Your response code is **BKS**.

Extra Helpings of Chicken Soup

Chicken Soup for the Surviving Soul
101 Stories of Courage and Inspiration from Those Who Have Survived Cancer

For years, the uplifting stories in the *Chicken Soup for the Soul* series have empowered individuals who have serious illnesses. Now Jack Canfield and Mark Victor Hansen have joined with Patty Aubery and Nancy Mitchell for a special batch of *Chicken Soup* devoted to stories of people beating cancer and finding renewed meaning in their lives.

Code 4029 trade paperback $12.95
Code 4037 hardcover $24.00

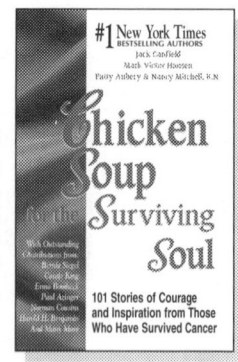

Chicken Soup for the Soul™ Cookbook
101 Stories with Recipes from the Heart

Here authors Jack Canfield and Mark Victor Hansen have teamed up with award-winning cookbook author Diana von Welanetz Wentworth and dished up a delightful collection of stories accompanied by mouthwatering recipes.

Code 3545 trade paperback $16.95
Code 3634 hardcover $29.95

Sopa de pollo para el alma
(Spanish Language Version)
Relatos que conmueven el corazón y ponen fuego en el espíritu

The national bestseller and 1995 ABBY Award winner *Chicken Soup for the Soul* is now available in a lovingly prepared Spanish language edition. The stories found in *Sopa de pollo para el alma* are as rich as mole sauce and as robust and invigorating as café Cubano.

Code 3537 trade paperback. $12.95

Available at your favorite bookstore or call 1-800-441-5569 for Visa or MasterCard orders. Prices do not include shipping and handling. Your response code is **BKS**.